WONG KAR-WAI'S
Ashes
of Time

We thank Xu Bing for writing Hong Kong University Press in his Square Word Calligraphy for t[...]of this book[...]rther expla[...]ee p. iv.

*'I would prefer ashes as the better paradigm for what I call the trace —
something that erases itself totally, radically, while presenting itself.'*

- Jacques Derrida

'My movies have nothing to do with deconstruction.'

- Wong Kar-wai

WONG KAR-WAI'S
Ashes of Time

Wimal Dissanayake

with

Dorothy Wong

香港大學出版社
HONG KONG UNIVERSITY PRESS

Hong Kong University Press
14/F Hing Wai Centre
7 Tin Wan Praya Road
Aberdeen
Hong Kong

www.hkupress.org
(secure on-line ordering)

© Hong Kong University Press 2003

ISBN 962 209 584 4 (Hardback)
ISBN 962 209 585 2 (Paperback)

British Library Cataloguing-in-Publication Data
A catalogue record for this book is available from the British Library.

Printed and bound by Condor Production Ltd., Hong Kong, China

Hong Kong University Press is honoured that Xu Bing, whose
art explores the complex themes of language across cultures,
has written the Press's name in his Square Word Calligraphy.
This signals our commitment to cross-cultural thinking and the
distinctive nature of our English-language books published in
China.

"At first glance, Square Word Calligraphy appears to be nothing
more unusual than Chinese characters, but in fact it is a new
way of rendering English words in the format of a square so they
resemble Chinese characters. Chinese viewers expect to be able
to read Square Word Calligraphy but cannot. Western viewers,
however are surprised to find they can read it. Delight erupts
when meaning is unexpectedly revealed."

— Britta Erickson, *The Art of Xu Bing*

Contents

Series Preface   vii

Acknowledgments   xi

1 Introduction   1

2 Background   5

3 Story   23

4 Characters   35

5 Narrative Structure   47

6 Style   59

7 Martial Arts   75

8 Time   97

9   Melancholia   109

10   Fragmentation   119

11   Response   129

12   Conclusion   139

Appendix 1   149

Appendix 2   159

Notes   161

Filmography   167

Selected Bibliography   171

Series Preface

The New Hong Kong cinema came into existence under very special circumstances, during a period of social and political crisis resulting in a change of cultural paradigms. Such critical moments have produced the cinematic achievements of the early Soviet cinema, neorealism, the 'nouvelle vague', the German cinema in the 70s and, we can now say, the recent Hong Kong cinema. If this cinema grew increasingly intriguing in the 1980s, after the announcement of Hong Kong's return to China, it was largely because it had to confront a new cultural and political space that was both complex and hard to define, where the problems of colonialism were overlaid with those of globalism in an uncanny way. Such uncanniness could not be caught through straight documentary or conventional history writing; it was left to the cinema to define it.

It does so by presenting to us an urban space that slips away if we try to grasp it too directly, a space that cinema coaxes into existence by whatever means at its disposal. Thus it is by eschewing a narrow idea of relevance and pursuing disreputable genres like melodrama, kung fu and the fantastic that cinema brings into view something else about the city which could otherwise be missed.

One classic example is Stanley Kwan's *Rouge*, which draws on the unrealistic form of the ghost story to evoke something of the uncanniness of Hong Kong's urban space. It takes a ghost to catch a ghost.

In the new Hong Kong cinema, then, it is neither the subject matter nor a particular generic conventions that is paramount. In fact, many Hong Kong films begin by following generic conventions but proceed to transform them. Such transformation of genre is also the transformation of a sense of place where all the rules have quietly and deceptively changed. It is this shifting sense of place, often expressed negatively and indirectly — but in the best work always rendered precisely in (necessarily) innovative images — that is decisive for the New Hong Kong Cinema.

Has the creative period of the New Hong Kong Cinema come to an end? However we answer the question, here is a need now to evaluate the achievements of Hong Kong cinema. During the last few years, a number of full-length books have appeared, testifying to the topicality of the subject. These books survey the field with varying degrees of success, but there is yet an almost complete lack of authoritative texts focusing in depth on individual Hong Kong films. This book series on the New Hong Kong Cinema is designed to fill this lack. Each volume will be written by a scholar/critic who will analyse each chosen film in detail and provide a critical apparatus for further discussion including filmography and bibliography.

Our objective is to produce a set of interactional and provocative readings that would make a self-aware intervention into modern Hong Kong culture. We advocate no one theoretical position; the authors will approach their chosen films from their own distinct points of vantage and interest. The aim of the series is to generate open-ended discussions of the selected films, employing diverse analytical strategies, in order to urge the readers towards self-reflective engagements with the films in particular and the

Hong Kong cultural space in general. It is our hope that this series will contribute to the sharpening of Hong Kong culture's conceptions of itself.

In keeping with our conviction that film is not a self-enclosed signification system but an important cultural practice among similar others, we wish to explore how films both reflect and inflect culture. And it is useful to keep in mind that reflection of reality and realty of reflection are equally important in the understanding of cinema.

Ackbar Abbas
Wimal Dissanayake

Series General Editors

Acknowledgments

We wish to thank Shu Kei for sharing with us his first-hand knowledge of *Ashes of Time*. We are deeply grateful to Ackbar Abbas, Jeremy Tambling, Lo Kwai-cheung , Dawn Tsang, Rosemary Wong and Ng Chin-pang as well as the four anonymous readers of the Hong Kong University Press for their valuable suggestions. The essay is better for their kindness. They are, of course, not responsible for any errors and failures that may be found in the ensuing pages. We are also very grateful to Doreen Dissanayake for her advice. It must be stated categorically that without the incredible energy and enthusiasm of Mina Cerny Kumar of the Hong Kong University Press, this book would not have seen the light of day. We are also in debt of the Press for the careful editing of the manuscript. We would also like to thank Block 2 Pictures Inc., for permission to reprint the film stills, and the Hong Kong Film Archive for providing the prints.

Wimal Dissanayake wishes to thank the Freemason Trust for supporting his work on Asian Cinema.

This book was written before the death of Leslie Cheung whose contribution to Hong Kong Cinema is immense.

1

Introduction

Ashes of Time (Dongxie Xidu) by Wong Kar-wai was made in 1994. It is a martial arts movie, loosely based on the popular novel, *Eagle-shooting Heroes* by Louis Cha (Jin Yong). It took two years to make and cost 47 million Hong Kong dollars. Wong Kar-wai himself wrote the screenplay. Christopher Doyle is the cinematographer and William Chang is the art director. These three people form a well-known trio, having worked in some other films such as *Chungking Express*, *Fallen Angels* and *Happy Together*. The cast consists of eight of the most popular actors and actresses in Hong Kong — Leslie Cheung, Tony Leung Kar-fai, Brigitte Lin Ching-hsia, Tony Leung Chui-wai, Maggie Cheung, Jacky Cheung, Carina Lau and Charlie Young. The celebrated martial arts instructor Sammo Hung choreographed the fight sequences.

Despite this highly esteemed cast and the reputation of Wong Kar-wai as an innovative film director, the film was not a commercial success. Initially, even the critical views were of a mixed nature. However, over the years, the weight of critical opinion has shifted and has begun to support the film and make important claims for it. It is a visually remarkable film, and even its most unforgiving critics admit this fact.

It is our conviction that *Ashes of Time* is a very significant film and that it marks an important point in the growth of Hong Kong cinema. Our interpretation of the film has been powered by this conviction. Although Wong himself has stated that in making this film he was inspired by John Ford's *The Searchers*, the connections between the two are somewhat tenuous. We have sought to discuss what we consider are important aspects of the text as well as a number of other related topics that we hope would illuminate the film, including the response of viewers. In the appendix, we have included excerpts from interviews given by Wong Kar-wai himself as well as by the director of music, the art director and the editors, in the hope that they would add further to our understanding of the film. Some of these were originally published in Chinese newspapers and journals, which would ordinarily be unavailable to English readers. Dorothy Wong translated these materials from the original Chinese.

Wong Kar-wai is not an easy director to engage with. He shuns facile connections and stereotypes. He is not a director who encourages reading his works in a hurry; his films need time — time for reconfiguration and time for reflection. He discourages ready-made categories and pigeon-holes into which his films might be quickly inserted. He wants us to respond to his films as a distinctly and independently evolving corpus, intertextually connected, and not as examples of prefabricated categories. As a filmmaker, Wong Kar-wai is not afraid to break rules. That is because he takes rules with the utmost seriousness. He is a difficult filmmaker because his ambiguous style resists easy comprehesion, a style resulting from disjunctions between narratives and images, and signifiers and referents. The lexical slippages as well as his self-referential aesthetic and his frequent practice of making the creation of the film itself the object of a metacommentary add to the difficulties. The density and intensity of the visual registers, and the shifting meanings within them, can be demanding, even enigmatic. His films lead to other films by him, thereby making each of his films a reflection or extension of the others. Each of his films is in continual dialogue with his other works. *Ashes of Time*, which, like many of his other films, puts into play the memory of ruins and the ruins of memory, adds to the panorama of futility that obsesses him and adds to the complex dignity of cinematic art. In his films, Wong is not interested in creatively mapping life as it is or should be. His concern is with mapping life as it brushes against the senses and intellect. Wong Kar-wai is a name that signifies simultaneously success and failure in the realm of Hong Kong cinema. This book will explain some of the reasons why this is so.

In this book, we have sought to examine *Ashes of Time* in relation to the creativity of Wong Kar-wai. One does not have to be a staunch supporter of the auteur theory to recognize the importance of this director in filmmaking. At the same time, we have tried to pay equal attention to the historical, social, cultural discourses that inflect his creativity. In any case, looking back on the development of film hermeneutics during the past four decades, it becomes evident that the battles between the proponents and opponents of the auteur theory were largely irrelevant. We think the concept of signature and countersignature proposed by Jacques Derrida is far more relevant to the issue of authorship. Derrida points out that a signature needs a countersignature, and most often the countersignature precedes the signature. By countersignature he means the 'conventions, institutions, processes of legitimization'[1] that are vital to the foregrounding of authorship. Hence, while focusing on *Ashes of Time* as the work of Wong Kar-wai, we have sought to locate it in the larger social, cultural, historical and conceptual contexts which it both reflects and inflects.

Many viewers have stated that *Ashes of Time* is a difficult film.

It is a difficult film not because we cannot derive a meaning from it but rather because we are compelled to derive more meanings than we can comfortably handle. The way Wong Kar-wai translates lives into images demand close scrutiny. How he converses with reality and reads society has implications that go beyond the perimeter of his personal reference; it has deeper social and cultural resonances. His films demand multifaceted readings. For example, the problematic interconnections of time and memory and the complex ways in which memory constitutes and de-constitutes characters in *Ashes of Time* invite the kind of detailed analysis that we cannot undertake in this short book. Freud's confession that 'no psychological theory has yet succeeded in giving a connected account of the fundamental phenomenon of remembering and forgetting' only underscores the impossibility of examining these topics successfully within a brief compass.

In the following pages we have sought to broach a number of what we think are important facets of the film. Again, given the brevity of the book, we can only hint at certain lines of inquiry and angles of exploration that could be productively pursued but it is impossible to do full analytical justice to them. While writing this book, we were reminded of Oscar Wilde's quip that 'there are two ways of disliking art ... One is to dislike it. The other is to like it rationally.'

2

Background

Wong Kar-wai is a filmmaker who is closely associated with the second phase of the New Wave in Hong Kong cinema. However, while he shares many features in common with the second phase New Wave film directors, he is also different from them and stands out with his signature traits. While his own films share many features in common, and constitute an evolving oeurve, *Ashes of Time* is also different from the rest of his works. A recognition of these similarities and differences opens the doorway to understanding *Ashes of Time* and locating it in its true discursive context.

Hong Kong has had a vibrant film industry for many decades. Hong Kong's growing economy and increasing recognition as an international financial center was conducive to film production, as clearly seen in the 1970s and 1980s. According to film historians, *To Steal a Roasted Duck* was the first narrative film made in Hong Kong. The film was directed by Liang Shaobo and produced by the American theatre owner Benjamin Polanski in 1909. Since that date, the Hong Kong film industry has grown rapidly — with a few ups and downs — and confronted new challenges and shaped itself in response to them. The people of Hong Kong are enamoured of their movies, and it was said that there have been years when as many as three hundred films were made in a year in this tiny territory.

The Hong Kong film industry and film culture received a substantial impetus from film industry workers from China who migrated from the Mainland both before and during World War II. Those who were bent on making films in Cantonese were impelled by a variety of motives and were quick to take advantage of the financial resources available in Hong Kong. Some made films with the objective of defying Japanese aggression, while others were reacting against the Guomindang government's decree that Mandarin should be the medium of all films. From the perspective of the present essay, another important reason was the banning of martial arts films by the Guomindang in the 1930s because they were perceived to be reactionary glorifications of feudal ways of life that hampered social progress. As a consequence of these trends, the late 1940s witnessed a sharp rise in the number of Cantonese films that were produced in Hong Kong. It was only a decade earlier, in 1933, when the first sound Cantonese film was produced. When one charts the evolution of Hong Kong's film industry and film culture, the crucial role played by the Shaw Brothers and Golden Harvest studios becomes readily apparent. It is to the credit of these two institutions that they were able to secure a firm industrial footing for film and turn it into an important segment of popular culture in Hong Kong.

When moviegoers outside of Hong Kong think of Hong Kong cinema, they automatically think of martial arts (kung fu) films because kung fu has become so closely identified with the film culture of Hong Kong. This is, of course, a misleading picture. There were other works of cinema made in the territory that display diverse styles and techniques which seek to explore a variety of themes and experiences. The martial arts film grew out of its deep roots in traditional Chinese culture, however, as the genre evolved, directors sought to challenge, absorb and undermine new social forces such as modernization, resulting in interesting trends. The kung fu film began to emerge as a distinctively Hong Kong art form with the production of the Huang Feihung series in the 1950s. The efforts of such artists as Zhang Che, Wang Yu, King Hu, Bruce Lee, Ng See-yuen, Liu Chia-ling, Yuen Woo-ping, Sammo Hung, Jackie Chan, Tsui Hark, and Wong Kar-wai resulted in its diverse growth. The view of many critics that the majority of martial arts films are designed to provide trivial and escapist fantasies for most filmgoers is indeed true. However, it must also be recognized that filmmakers like King Hu and Zhang Che have used it with great imagination to create memorable experiences as in *A Touch of Zen*. Two filmmakers who have used this genre with much skill to attain serious artistic purposes and to raise important issues related to nationalism, imperialism, cultural modernity and technology are Tsui Hark and Wong Kar-wai. The latter's *Ashes of Time* is the subject of this study.

It must be noted that during the last fifteen years or so, a distinct form of Hong Kong cinema that seeks to combine elements of the popular and the artistic traditions has made its appearance. Film directors such as Tsui Hark, John Woo, Stanley Kwan and Wong Kar-wai represent this tradition. As Ackbar Abbas pointed out, 'The new Hong Kong cinema is interesting ... not essentially because it has caught up in terms of technical competence and sophistication with the rest of the world; what is really interesting about it is the way film is being used to explore and negotiate a problematic and paradoxical cultural space without abandoning its role as popular entertainment.'[1]

In order to understand the evolution of the New Wave in Hong Kong cinema it is perhaps useful to see it in two phases. The first phase started in 1979 and soon after a number of innovative films were produced. Among them Ann Hui's *The Secret*, Alan Fong's *Father and Son*, Patrick Tam's *Nomad*, Tony Au's *Last Affair*, and

Yim Ho's *Homecoming* deserve special mention. In the first phase of the New Wave films, the emphasis was on capturing a slice of reality. Instead of stereotypical characters and melodramatic story lines, the New Wave film directors focused on social issues of consequence. The second phase of the New Wave began in the late 1980s. Works such as Mabel Cheung's *An Autumn's Tale*, Clara Law's *Autumn Moon*, Stanley Kwan's *Rouge*, Lawrence Ah Mon's *Queen of Temple Street* and Wong Kar-wai's *As Tears Go By* represent the second phase. These film directors sought to combine the essence of the artistic and popular traditions in Hong Kong filmmaking with the avant-garde films of the West to create a new and vigorous form of cinema.

No film movement emerges out of a social vacuum. All film innovations bear the traces of specific social and cultural contexts that they inhabit. The period between 1984–97, in which much of the exciting work of the New Wave directors in Hong Kong was accomplished, was also a period which was vitally connected with the handover of Hong Kong to mainland China. The year 1984 marked the signing of the Sino-British declaration announcing the return of Hong Kong to China and 1997 was the year of the return. This was a period characterized by complex emotions of anxiety, hope, worry, uncertainty, national pride and a sense of loss. Any evaluation of the films made during this period cannot afford to ignore the social anxieties and the emotional qualities of this period. They relate in interesting and complex ways to the content of the films. In addition, one has to keep in mind the interactions between global capital, local culture and the transnational space that Hong Kong cinema has opened up. The financing, production, consumption and distribution of films as well as international film circuits, and the defining alterity of Hollywood have to be taken into consideration in assessing modern Hong Kong cinema.

It is against this background that one has to examine Wong Kar-wai's films in general and his *Ashes of Time* in particular.

Wong Ka-wai was born in Shanghai in 1958. He came to Hong Kong in 1963 with his parents. He spoke only Shanghainese and hence encountered great difficulties in adjusting to the Cantonese-speaking environment of Hong Kong. Initially he studied graphic design at Hong Kong Polytechnic University and displayed an interest in photography. In 1980 he enrolled in the training program for television drama production at TVB. Before long he emerged as a scriptwriter. He wrote over 50 scripts although only about 10 carry his name. The first film that he directed was *As Tears Go By* which was made in 1988 — it is a film that brings to mind Martin Scorsese's *Mean Streets*. He was the writer and director of the film. It is an exploration into the gangster genre. His intention, though, was to deglamorize the genre and lay bare the waste and violence that are endemic to gang life. The film deals with a gangster named Ah Wah in the rough neighborhood of Mong Kok. He is the guide and protector of his younger friend Fly. Fly is clumsy, making Ah Wah's life in the crime syndicate more complicated. Ah Wah's life is further complicated because of his affair with a distant cousin who wants him to forsake the violent life of a gangster. Wong Kar-wai explores this situation through striking imagery to deconstruct the very form of gangster movies.

Wong Kar-wai's second film, *Days of Being Wild*, was made in 1991 and gained wide critical recognition. The story, as in many of his films, is set in the 1960s. It portrays a young man named Yuddy who is given to violence and has an affair with two women. He later abandons them and goes off to the Philippines looking for his birth mother. Yuddy is a wealthy, carefree man who is confused and confuses others. He is an egotist who is afraid of entering into deep human relationships. His fears, anxieties and alienation can be explained by the fact that he grew up in an environment devoid of maternal love. His biological mother left for the Philippines and does not wish to see him, while his adoptive mother is an irresponsible alcoholic. This film highlights, in terms of content, some of the themes expressed in his later films — including *Ashes of Time* — such as alienation, solitude, fear of rejection, and rootlessness. His trademark style features fragmentation, episodic narration, discrepant spatial and temporal registers, the frequent use of voice-overs and the stressing of the visual over the verbal. There was to be a second part to this film but, because of the commercial failure of the first part, the project was abandoned. *Days of Being Wild* juxtaposes the feel of the 1960s with the pulse of the 1990s in an interesting way. In 1994 Wong Kar-wai made his third film, *Ashes of Time*. In the same year, in between the filming of *Ashes of Time*, Wong made his third film, *Chungking Express* (Chongqing Senlin), which became both a commercial and critical success. It is a light-hearted comedy unlike his other three films. It won for itself, not only financial success, but also widespread critical acclaim. The film deals with two loosely connected stories about two policemen abandoned by their girlfriends. In the first story, Takeshi Kaneshiro on his birthday goes to a bar firmly resolved to fall in love with the first woman he chances to meet. As luck would have it, he picks up a heroine smuggler wearing a blonde wig, played by Brigitte Lin. The second story deals with Tony Leung whose ex-girlfriend has left her keys at a fast food restaurant. He is so caught up in his own dejection that he fails to realize that the girl at the counter, who is interested in him, is stealthily redecorating his flat in his absence. Wong makes use of this somewhat strange story to focus on aspects of capitalist modernity in Hong Kong. The action of the film takes place in the famous Chungking Mansions, which have come to epitomize the hubris, crass consumerism and the throw-away culture associated with capitalist modernity.

In the same year, Wong Kar-wai also made *Ashes of Time*. Following this film, which was a commercial failure but a critical success, he made *Fallen Angels* (Duoluo Tianshi) in 1995. It was originally conceptualized as a sequel to *Chungking Express* and bears similarities in terms of style and visual rhetoric. *Fallen Angels* deals with the lives of a number of characters from the underworld of Hong Kong. They comprise a hit man and daring ex-convict who runs businesses at night. The film once again focuses on the modernized world of Hong Kong. The film contains many elements that we have now come to associate with the work of Wong. Moreover, the intertextual and self-referential qualities of the film give it added interest. A woman dyeing her hair blond, a character eating a can of pineapples which has already expired, a woman in a flight attendant's uniform nervously awaiting the arrival of her lover, and a fast food restaurant called 'Midnight Express' all recall episodes from *Chungking Express.*

In 1997 Wong Kar-wai made *Happy Together* (Chungguang Zhaxie), a story set in Argentina. This won for him the director's prize at the Cannes Film Festival. The film is subtitled, 'A Story About Reunion'. The film deals with the aftermath of the break up of a relationship between two gay men. It also contains interesting pointers to the handover of Hong Kong to mainland China. The film stars Leslie Cheung and Tony Leung Chiu-wai as lovers and stirred up controversy among certain groups. Loosely based on a somewhat obscure novel by Manuel Puig, this film explores a favorite theme of Wong's — the ambiguities of intimacy. As in many other films of his, popular songs provide a kind of frame of intelligibility. Being 'happy together' is a central topic of the film, but the film also shows the impossibility of this goal. The narrative of the film commences with the voice-over of Lai Yiu-fai, who confesses to us about his continuing relationship with Ho Po-wing. Both of them have come to Buenos Aires, halfway around the world, to see the famous Iguazu waterfalls, which stand as a dominating and controlling symbol in the film. During their travels they argue, bicker, break up and experience immense agony. Having been separated for a while, Ho Po-wing says, 'Let's start over again.' What the film repeatedly demonstrates is the impossibility of that undertaking. Nostalgia, and the problems of intimacy that are depicted in many of Wong's other films find echoes in *Happy Together* as well. If *As Tears Go By* can be termed a gangster movie, and *Ashes of Time* a martial arts movie, *Happy Together* may be regarded as a road movie. In all three cases, of course, the director undercuts the genre from within.

In 2000, Wong Kar-wai made his latest film, *In the Mood for Love* (Huayang Nianhua). It can be described as his most delicate film in terms of emotion and eroticism. The story is set in Hong Kong of the early 1960s. Tony Leung Chiu-wai and Maggie Cheung play next door neighbors. They are attracted to each other almost immediately. However, it is only after they realize that their spouses are involved in an affair that they decide to spend time together. The film can best be described as a study of sexual desire and its tensions, tenderness, ambiguities and repressions. The nostalgia for the 1960s that pervades the film is very real and compelling. We see in this film, as in many others, the organizing role played by dominant symbols. The telephone booth in *Days of Being Wild*, the birdcage in *Ashes of Time*, the waterfall in *Happy Together* and the carefully photographed walls in *In the Mood for Love* are cases in point.

What we have sought to do, through this quick survey of Wong Kar-wai's films, is to situate *Ashes of Time* in the larger context of his total oeuvre and the social and intellectual currents of the time. Unlike most other filmmakers, Wong's works are connected to each other in complex and subtle ways. Wong's early films offer useful pointers to the understanding of later films, while his later films enable us to revisit the earlier works with a new eye. Hence, in our effort to understand the nature and significance of *Ashes of Time*, it is of the utmost importance that we relate its themes, topics, tropes and visuals to those of his other films. The idea of simultaneously celebrating and indicting existence runs through all of his films. Let us, for example, consider the theme of self-deception that finds articulation in many of Wong's works. This theme certainly figures very prominently in *Ashes of Time*. Raphael Demos, in his seminal article, characterizes self-deception as follows: 'Self-deception exists, I will say, when a person lies to himself, that is to say, persuades himself to believe what he knows is not so. In short, self-deception entails that B believes both P and not-P at the same time.'[2] In our view, Demos is here focusing attention on a significant aspect of self-deception and not its totality. Explorations into self-deception should come to grips with questions of consciousness, rationality and irrationality, cognition, cognitive relativism, categories of belief, epistemic foundations, wish-fulfillment, structures of desire, incontinence, hypocrisy, irony, rhetoric of self-justification and others. In other words, it is a many-sided concept. Wong Kar-wai's characters often succumb to it. For example, Ouyang Feng believes that he has transformed himself into a new person and obliterated his past, when in fact neither is the case. Huang Yaoshi thinks he visits his friend Ouyang annually in the spring to renew acquaintances when in fact it allows him the opportunity to meet Ouyang's former girlfriend with whom he is in love. Murong Yin creates her alter ego Murong Yang as a way of transcending herself only to plunge even deeper into herself. Hence, self-deception is a recurrent theme in *Ashes of Time*. It is also a theme that finds articulation in his later works like *Happy Together* and *In the Mood for Love*. In *Happy Together*, the two estranged lovers believe that they can start all over again while fully realizing the impossibility of that undertaking. Similarly Tony Leung Chiu-wai and Maggie Cheung in *In the Mood for Love* repress their sexual desires and overtly pursue an ideal of pure love knowing full well the implications of their behaviour. Hence self-deception forms a part of the meaning of these two later films by Wong. What is interesting to note here is that our understanding of how self-deception works in *Ashes of Time* enables us to develop a more comprehensive framework of cognition to comprehend the dynamic between the two pairs of lovers in *Happy Together* and *In the Mood for Love*. In this way, *Ashes of Time* gains meaning when we connect it to the earlier and later works of Wong. It is for these reasons that we decided to locate *Ashes of Time* in the totality of his oeuvre.

When one considers *Ashes of Time* against the backdrop of his total output, interesting thematic patterns and pointers begin to emerge which are useful in decoding the meaning of the film. For example in *Ashes of Time*, the pair Ouyang and Huang are introduced very early and constitute an interesting duality. Similarly, in *As Tears Go By*, the Big Brother and his minion, in *Days of Being Wild*, Yuddy and the sailor, and in *Fallen Angels*, the assassin and his helpmate, in *Chungking Express*, the two policemen and their paramours, in *Happy Together*, the two gay lovers and *In the Mood for Love*, the man and woman in love and their spouses constitute similar dualities. In each of these films, Wong sets up these pairs, these dualities, only to subvert the binary logic.

The background to *Ashes of Time* involves social and cultural discourses, historical moments and conceptual as well as aesthetic spaces. It is not only the social background that one has to examine in considering the background to a film. For example, the aesthetic informing *Ashes of Time* has to be looked at in relation to his other works. It seems to us that the aesthetic that governs many of his films can be characterized as an aesthetic of difference. This operates at a number of levels of artistic understanding. For example, Wong makes use of different genres — gangster films, love stories, martial arts movies, road movies — only to subvert them from within. In other words, Wong's intention is to display his films' differences from the conventional forms. Similarly, he makes use of the aura surrounding the actors and actresses such as Leslie Cheung, Tony Leung Chiu-wai and Maggie Cheung to invigorate their performances. But in doing so, he also underlines the fact that their roles are different entities from themselves. Indeed there is a very intriguing ambivalence at work here. Moreover, the very semiotics used in Wong's films gain their vitality through their differences from their avowed intentions. This touches on the question of self-deception that we referred to earlier. Characters in *Ashes of Time* such as Ouyang, Huang, Murong Yang, the Sunset Warrior and Ouyang's sister-in-law think that they are occupying spaces, following emotional trajectories and pursuing cognitive maps that are, in point of fact, are different from what they understand them to be. Moreover, to add another layer of complexity, the film is different from itself, thereby making it inevitable that to seize the film is to lose it. We earlier emphasized the importance of recognizing the complex and evolving unity of Wong Kar-wai's cinematic output. However, it is important to take note of the fact that difference presupposes sameness and continuity; the experience of the continuum is also the experience of difference. Hence, it is against the background of similarities and continuities among Wong's works that one has to discover and identify the differences. In our judgment, then, the aesthetic of difference opens an interesting window onto the textual terrain of *Ashes of Time* as well as his other films. The depictions of continuity and difference set in motion a dynamic that forms a vital part of the conceptual and aesthetic background of Wong's films. One obvious difference that we need to bear in mind is that *Ashes of Time* is his only period-costume drama to date. While the stories in all his other films take place in the late 20th century's consumer, metropolitan societies, the story of *Ashes of Time* takes place in a remote desert around the 10th century.

In discussing the background of *Ashes of Time*, it is important that we focus on the state of the film industry at the time. We made a few references to the nature of the industry earlier on in this chapter. From the 1980s to mid–1990s, the Hong Kong film industry was making steady progress and inspiring investor confidence in the ability of Hong Kong's cinema to thrive as a commercial proposition. For example, during this period box office collections from locally made films far outpaced that of foreign films, including those from Hollywood. Just to give a representative example, in 1984, of the 22 most popular movies shown in Hong Kong, 20 were made in Hong Kong itself. It is interesting to note that *Raiders of the Lost Ark*, which grossed the largest amount of money among foreign films, was beaten in the popular ratings by five other films made in Hong Kong. The second most popular foreign film that year, the James Bond movie *Never Say Never Again* was only the 14th most popular film. This gives us a sense of how local films were performing in relation to foreign films.

In the years 1990, 1991 and 1993, 247, 211 and 234 films were made in Hong Kong, respectively. While in 1997 and 1998, the figure dropped sharply to 94 and 92, respectively. During the past six years or so, foreign films have begun to make more money than locally produced films. This period witnessed a catastrophic drop in both output and investment. A number of factors contributed to this deplorable situation. The popularity of forms of low-cost, in-home entertainment (including VCD's), piracy and lax enforcement of intellectual property laws, increasing popularity of American movies, the incorporation of Hong Kong film styles and techniques by American producers in the action-film genre, rising ticket prices and the consequent drop in movie attendance, and the difficulties encountered in competing with big-budget Hollywood films are some of the reasons for the decline in Hong Kong's film industry.

The following figures indicate the nature of the change over a ten-year period. The box office collections are given in HK$ millions.

	Local Box Office of *Hong Kong Films*	*Local Box Office of* *Non-Hong Kong Films*
1990	936	468
1991	994	294
1992	1,240	312
1993	1,133	406
1994	957	427
1995	776	563
1996	659	563
1997	548	608
1998	422	544
1999	353	523
2000	383	531

During the period in which *Ashes of Time* was made, Hong Kong's film industry, as is seen in the figures above, was still commercially vibrant. As a consequence, filmmakers such as Wong Kar-wai were able to make innovative films that took risks and *Ashes of Time* is certainly a good example of this. There were 192 films made in Hong Kong in 1994 — the year in which *Ashes of Time* was made. It was a big budget film featuring a large number of some of the most well-known actors and actresses in the territory. However, it was not commercially successful. It was number 34 in the popularity chart, grossing around HK$9 million. The ten most popular films that year were *God of Gamblers' Return, Drunken Master II, From China with Love, It's a Wonderful Life, Treasure, Love on Delivery, Hail the Judge, He's a Woman, She's a Man, I Have a Date with Spring* and *In Between*.

In discussing the background to *Ashes of Time* it is also important that we pay some attention to its production history. The story of the making of *Ashes of Time* is, in many ways, as interesting as the film itself, filled with tension, anxiety, despair and ultimately, relief. *Ashes of Time* was presented by the Taiwan-based Scholar Films Company Limited. It was a Jet Tone Production in association with Tsui Ming Productions Limited, Beijing Film Studio and Pony Canyon Inc. The Scholar Film Company, which was responsible for the funding, was interested in making two films based on the popular series of novels *Eagle-shooting Heroes* by Jin Yong. The two films were to be different from one another; one a serious and artistic film and the other a more popular comedy, a parody of the martial arts form. Wong Kar-wai was to be responsible for the artistic film and Jeff Lau for the more popular one. From the 1980s onwards, the Scholar Films Company had made a reputation for itself as a high-powered production and exhibition company.

At that time, as it is in many ways now, the common practice among Hong Kong producers was to pre-sell their products in Taiwan and Southeast Asian countries such as Singapore and Malaysia before the films were made, on the basis of the story, the genre and the reputation of the cast and director. The producers of *Ashes of Time* followed suit, pre-selling it in Taiwan, Singapore, Malaysia and Korea. However, as the shooting began, it became evident to everyone concerned that the production costs were excessively high and continued to rise, and were going to be well over original estimates. The Scholar Films Company became deeply anxious.

It was at this time that the well-known film critic, filmmaker and distributor, Shu Kei was called on to mount a rescue operation. (He is also responsible for the English subtitles in the film). He was successful in pre-selling the film in France and Japan and raising about half-a-million American dollars from each of the two countries. One of the conditions imposed by the Japanese was that Pony Canyon (Japan) should be credited as one of the producers. However, as the making of the film progressed, and with it the mounting costs, this money was quickly used up and the Scholar

Film Company had to pump in more. Ultimately, the film was made; but there were several moments of intense anxiety regarding the viability of the project.

Ashes of Time gained international recognition in the ensuing years. Its showing at the Venice Film Festival in 1994 greatly aided this recognition as a visually remarkable film. The chain of events leading to its showing in the Venice Film Festival is an interesting story by itself, shedding light on Wong Kar-wai's work habits, intensity and priorities as a film director. Marco Muller, the representative of the Venice Film Festival, saw parts of a version of the film edited by William Chang, and was greatly impressed by it. He recommended it to the Festival Organizers and a date was set for it to be shown to the panel. An unsubtitled tape of this version was sent to Italy for the committee to view. The director of the Venice film festival, Gillo Pontecorvo, decided to invite the film for competition. But a week later, he changed his mind and decided that the committee should see the final edited version before they could accept the film. However, Wong Kar-wai was constantly making changes to it, re-editing and seeking to give the story a sharper focus, so he could not meet the deadline. The organizers decided to extend the date; but Wong still could not make it because he was busy with last minute changes that he thought would add to the effect of the film. The Festival was to start soon and the organizers demanded that the film has to arrive by the first day of the festival, or else it would not be shown. It was decided that the film be taken to Venice by hand. The organizers as well as the producers were getting more and more worried, while Wong was still doing the final touches. All the reels except the last were given to the courier. The courier was at the airport awaiting the final reel while Wong was still working on it. Finally, just minutes before the airplane took off, the final reel was delivered. There are similar stories that are revelatory of Wong Kar-wai's temperament and work style.

During the course of making the film, several important changes were made regarding casting as well as technical assistance. For example, Leslie Cheung was originally slated to play the role that Tony Leung Kar-fai ended up playing in the film and Tony Leung Kar-fai played Leslie Cheung's role. After some weeks of shooting, it was decided that they should switch roles. Similarly, according to the original plan, Charlie Young, who is a skilled martial arts performer, was to play the role of a ferocious horse thief instead of her present minor role in the film. Some sequences were shot of her playing the role of a horse thief, but later Wong decided to give her the minor role in the film. Joey Wong, who recently appeared in *The Peony Traveler*, appears in one shot in the last action montage. She was in the original cast when the film was pre-sold to Korea. Wong decided to drop her later but had to keep that shot in the final version released in Asia simply to fulfill his contractual obligations to the Korean distributors. *Ashes of Time* was originally assembled by Patrick Tam, but later William Chang was entrusted with the task of editing the film along with the help of Hai Kit-wai and Kwong Chi-leung. Similarly, Peter Pau, the cameraman behind *Crouching Tiger, Hidden Dragon* was the original cinematographer, and later Christopher Doyle took over.

Ashes of Time was released in 1994 and the general reaction to the film was one of bewilderment and disappointment. This was not the martial arts film that many had hoped to see. Despite the glamorous cast and the beautiful photography, many in the audience were less than enthusiastic about the film. They felt that it was over their heads. People walked out of the theatres in droves in the middle of the film and people from the industry were appalled. Critics like Shek Kei found the film perplexing. A few critics liked it, and there was a furious battle in the pages of newspapers and journals, between those who liked it and those who did not, with an intensity that had hardly been witnessed before. However, with the passage of time and partly due to the informed explanations of critics and scholars, as well as the impact Wong's later works had in generating intertextual energies, there emerged among some viewers a more favorable impression of *Ashes of Time* that was appreciative of the powerful, if flawed, imagination, and the vibrant, critical intelligence inscribed in it. This is the kind of film that grows on you. It must be seen more than once to understand its meaning. This point was well articulated by Maggie Cheung, who plays a significant, although a small role in terms of screen time, in *Ashes of Time*. She remarked in an interview, 'The first time I saw it I thought "What's it about?" But the second time I thought, "Actually it's quite good." And the third time I really loved it when I understood the meaning of the film.'

3

Story

Ouyang Feng (Malicious West, played by Leslie Cheung) is a
middle-aged swordsman living in the desert, separated from normal
society. When he was a young man, full of life and vitality, his desire
was to make a name for himself as a skillful and intrepid swordsman
and make a deep impression in the world of martial arts. He was
so bent on achieving his ambition that he left his native home, the
White Camel Mountain, leaving behind his girlfriend (Maggie
Cheung) to chase his dream. In sheer frustration, and as a way of
seeking revenge, the woman marries Ouyang's elder brother. This
marriage resulted in Ouyang deciding to live out the rest of his life
in exile. He retires to the desert and opens an inn. He then becomes
an agent for killers, hiring young and poor swordsmen with great
ambitions of becoming famous warriors to do the killing for him.
However, his solitary life has the effect of generating memories
from the life he left behind. Consequently, Ouyang becomes
apathetic, miserable, scheming and obsessed with money. The once
skillful swordsman with noble ambitions is now transformed into
a mercenary who kills for money.

Ouyang is visited every year by his friend Huang Yaoshi (Tony

Leung Kar-fai), who, like Ouyang, is burdened by sad memories of an unfortunate love affair. Huang once had an unconsummated affair with the wife of his best friend at Peach Blossom Island. Huang comes every year during the peach blossom season to drink with Ouyang. After that he goes to White Camel Mountain to pay a visit to Ouyang's former love. The woman now has a ten-year-old boy and her husband had died many years ago. Although she still thinks of her past with Ouyang fondly, she and Huang are in love with each other. During peach blossom season every year, Huang thinks about her. He uses his visit to Ouyang as an excuse to see her and brings her news about Ouyang's whereabouts and the kind of life he is destined to lead.

Once in Fusu city, Huang is befriended by a man named Murong Yang (Brigitte Lin). They get drunk together, and Huang half-facetiously promises to marry Murong Yang's sister, Murong Yin. They fix on a date to meet, but Huang does not show up. Murong Yang is upset and angry. He is perturbed by Huang's deception and insulting behaviour. Murong Yang then offers Ouyang a large sum of money to kill Huang. Knowing of this plot, the sister, Murong Yin, asks Ouyang to kill Murong Yang and save Huang. She is unhappy with her brother for forbidding her to be with Huang. Ouyang is confronted by a cruel dilemma. To make matters worse, Ouyang realizes that Murong Yang and Murong Yin are not two people, but one person, reminding us of Shakespeare's line in *Twelfth Night*, 'One face, one voice, one habit and two persons.' They represent the two warring personalities of the same person. The symbolism of yin and yang is obvious.

Murong's pertinacity finds an echo in a peasant girl (Charlie Young) who begs Ouyang to avenge the death of her brother. She cannot offer him vast sums of money; all she can give him in return is a mule and a basket of eggs. Money-minded Ouyang firmly rejects this request, but the girl is adamant and persistent, so he tells her to wait until someone arrives who might help her. At this point the

Sunset Warrior (Tony Leung Chiu-wai), also known as the Blind Swordsman, arrives on the scene. He is partially blind and his eyesight is deteriorating very rapidly. The Sunset Warrior offers to undertake a killing for money, so that he can journey back to Peach Blossom Island and see the peach blossoms for one last time before he surrenders himself to total darkness. He had resolved to become an itinerant swordsman because his wife fell in love with his best friend, who happens to be Huang Yaoshi. The Sunset Warrior could never forgive Huang for what he did. He then demonstrates his superb powers of swordsmanship by killing a proud warrior. Ouyang recruits the Sunset Warrior to slaughter a gang of horse thieves on behalf of the villagers who are harassed by them. However, the Sunset Warrior is killed in combat because of his near blindness. A year later, out of sheer curiosity, Ouyang decides to visit Peach Blossom Island. There he encounters a woman, Peach Blossom (Carina Lau), the Sunset Warrior's wife.

Ouyang becomes determined to eliminate the gang of robbers who were responsible for the death of the Sunset Warrior. To do this, he recruits another poverty-stricken swordsman by the name of Hong Qi (Jacky Cheung). Hong fervently hopes to become a famous swordsman. He is poor and is barefooted so Ouyang buys him a pair of shoes. Through his valour and skill, Hong is able to subdue his opponents and get rid of the entire gang. He also kills a group of swordsmen responsible for the death of the peasant girl's brother — a request previously turned down by Ouyang. Hong's decision to kill a man for the price of an egg infuriates Ouyang. Although in the fight Hong loses one of his fingers, he did not regret it because he has redeemed himself as a warrior. Hong does not agree with Ouyang's viewpoint that every task he does needs to have a commensurate financial reward. There are certain actions, he thinks, that need to be undertaken irrespective of the monetary gain.

The inhumanity of Ouyang is further illustrated in one of the scenes in *Ashes of Time*. When Hong's wife asks Ouyang to fetch a doctor to care for Hong, who is seriously ill, Ouyang rejects the request, saying that doctors cost money. After his wife (Bai Li) nurses Hong back to health, she insists that he bring her on his martial adventure. Even though it is not the custom for swordsmen to go adventuring with their wives, Hong agrees to her request because of her firm resolve in the matter. When the couple leaves, Ouyang feels envious.

The woman whom Ouyang once loved and had become his sister-in-law dies of a sickness. Before dying, she asks Huang to deliver a bottle of wine to Ouyang. This wine has the special property of making the people who drink it forget the past. She knows that Ouyang, in the deepest recesses of his heart, pines for her just as much as she does. After she presents this wine to Ouyang, Huang drinks from it, obliterating his memories of the past. However, Huang still remembers the woman he was hoping to marry but is now the wife of another. Six years later, Huang retreats to the Peach Blossom Island. There he lives a life of solitude and becomes known as the Malevolent East. Meanwhile, Ouyang receives a letter informing him of the death of his sister-in-law. The letter is signed by Ouyang Ke, someone who claims to be the woman's son. Ouyang leaves the desert and returns to White Camel Mountain. There he becomes known as the Malicious West.

This is the basic situation of the film, and it is deceptively banal. Memory plays a crucial role in the propulsion of the narrative: Wong Kar-wai seems to be saying that it is not the continuities but the discontinuities that evoke memory and, through memory, evoke the narrative discourse. The dialectic between memory and forgetfulness animates the narrative, and it is interesting to recall that Ouyang's former girlfriend sends him the wine of amnesia so that he can forget the past. As Maurice Blanchot once remarked, 'Memory is where forgetting breathes.'

Ashes of Time is based on Louis Cha's (Jin Yong's) *The Eagle-shooting Heroes*. It is a multi-volume novel that contains a rambling story about power, intrigue, and adventure against the backdrop of classical China. However, the film is not an adaptation as we normally understand the term. What the director/scriptwriter has done is to select a few characters from the original work. The film follows three middle-aged characters from the novel. They are Huang Yaoshi (Malevolent East), Ouyang Feng (Malicious West) and Hong Qi. The fourth important character that figures in the novel, Great Master Yi Deng, the Emperor of the South, is left out of the film. Furthermore, a comparison of the original novel and the film uncovers the fact that it is only Ouyang's story that closely follows the original work. The characters of Huang Yaoshi and Hong Qi are portrayed differently in the narrative of the novel. In addition, one has to take note of the fact that in Jin Yong's novel, the three characters — Huang Yaoshi, Ouyang Feng and Hong Qi — receive equal attention in terms of the narrative. However, the film's focus is on Ouyang and the other two characters are reduced to ancillary roles, taking up only a quarter of the narrative's time. Hence, the film *Ashes of Time* can be said to be loosely and selectively based on the *The Eagle-shooting Heroes*.

Jin Yong's *The Eagle-shooting Heroes* trilogy is extremely popular in Hong Kong, having made a deep impression on the thought and imagination of the people. During the past four decades, numerous television programs and films and plays have been made about these novels. However, the way the scriptwriter/ director, Wong Kar-wai, has made use of the novel is clearly different from the earlier efforts. When the film was first shown many viewers were confused and disappointed and some even walked out. This was largely because Wong Kar-wai was seeking to unsettle and challenge the images of the leading characters that had been etched into the imaginations of Hong Kong audiences. The broad parameters set by the novel and its martial arts form allowed the director the challenging task of working against expectations, and testing its limits.

Clearly, *Ashes of Time* is not an adaptation of *The Eagle-shooting Heroes*, neither in terms of the narrative nor fidelity to the original conception of the characters. Thinking of the film as a supplement, in the Derridean sense, may be more appropriate. It is both an extension and replacement of the original narrative. The three characters taken from the original work both extend their original profiles and also subvert them. The three characters are a means of allowing the scriptwriter/director, Wong Kar-wai, to give free rein to his imagination. The characters of Ouyang Feng, Huang Yaoshi and Hong Qi are in their old age in Jin Yong's novel. In *Ashes of Time* it seems as if the director is keen to provide us with a history of their younger and more active days. Hence, in terms of the narrative discourse, the film ends where the novel begins. Moreover, the conception of the characters in the original novel and the film are clearly different. For example, in the novel, Huang is depicted as handsome, gifted, intelligent and artistically inclined. He detests double standards and greatly appreciates loyalty. He is a man of solitude, but at the same time he is deeply fond of his family. When his wife dies while giving birth to his daughter, Huang is overwhelmed by unbearable sadness. He even thinks of killing himself and being buried along with his wife. However, he abandons this idea as he realizes that it is his duty to bring up his young daughter. The concept of Huang Yaoshi that emerges from the novel, therefore, is very different from the one articulated in the film.

Similarly, the character of Hong Qi that emerges from the pages of the original novel is at variance with his depiction in the film. In Jin Yong's novel, he is regarded and valued as the most eminent of the five masters of the martial arts world. He proclaims that he has slaughtered 231 people because each of them was immoral and villainous. He becomes the leader of the clan of mendicants; however, he hardly stays with his fellow mendicants, preferring instead to travel by himself and partake of good food. Hong is also known by the name 'Nine-Finger Mendicant'. This is due to his resolution to cut off his second finger as a form of self-punishment. Once again, we observe the discrepancies between the images of Hong in the novel and the film. Clearly, our aim is not to undertake a full-scale comparison of the novel and the film, which would be a different subject altogether and demand a different forum. Ours is the far more modest intention of hinting at some of the differences in the respective concepts of characters found in the novel and the film.

The story of *Ashes of Time* contains many elements found in Wong's other works such as *Days of Being Wild*, *As Tears Go By*, *Fallen Angels*, *Chungking Express*, *Happy Together* and *In the Mood for Love*. The sense of loneliness, the oppressive power of memory, the inability to communicate, the dislocations, disconnections and disappointments in love that are experienced by the characters are common to most of these films. *Ashes of Time* is a story of unrequited love as are the stories narrated in Wong's other films. It is as if Yeats' line, 'Our souls/ Are love, and a continual farewell' has deep implications for Wong as a storyteller. Ouyang Feng, Huang Yaoshi, the Sunset Warrior, Murong Yang and Ouyang's former girlfriend are victims of unrequited love. For them, love is always a postponement of happiness. They go through life carrying with them the burdens of sad and tormenting memories. Consequently, they hate the world they love.

The lack of communication or the inability to communicate and the subsequent loneliness that ensues is a vital part of the story of *Ashes of Time* as indeed in most of his other films. Wong Kar-wai's films reconfigure the complex and uncertain terrain of human intimacy in new and interesting ways, investing his films with a certain uneasy emotionality. In his films, intimacy arises not from couples coming together through love, but through their inability to do so. It is an intimacy of negation. The story of *Ashes of Time* is one of entanglement where each of the characters is involved, in one way or another, with the fortunes of the others. Each of the characters enters the private space of the others. However, one never gets the feeling that there is a deep sense of union, or a close empathy arising from productive communication among them. Hence, each of the characters is imprisoned in a world of their own making. Although they tell stories to each other, in a strange way it only reinforces that sense of solitude. Interestingly, the voice-overs that Wong Kar-wai used throughout the film only serve to fragment and not unify that world. Throughout the film, the director wants the world to recognize, as he does, the inevitability of fragmentation and difficulties of communication.

One is also left with the impression that there is cruel fate at work in the world that the characters in *Ashes of Time* inhabit. Much of the action of the story has already happened; they are now reduced to beings of memory. As Wong Kar-wai himself remarked, 'There's also another significant difference between *Ashes of Time* and my other films. With the latter, I'd start with the beginning of a story or certain characters, gradually working out the ending as the shoot went on. With *Ashes*, I had known the ending of these characters before I started and I could not change it. This has imbued a sense of fatalism in both me and the film.'

What is of particular interest about this story is the way presence and absence are played off each other — how presence in absence dominates the action. This is, of course, crucially linked to the nature of desire. The complexity of desire constitutes a theme of this film. Desire has to be understood as both fact and fiction. Hence, the crucial role of fantasy in the creation of desire. People desire most what is absent. Or to phrase it differently, absence is a precondition of desire. This is clearly seen in the characters of Ouyang Feng, his former girlfriend, Huang Yaoshi, Murong Yang and the Sunset Warrior. Roland Barthes raises the pertinent question, 'Is not desire always the same, whether the object is present or absent? Isn't the object always absent?'[1] This question has a pointed relevance to the themes in *Ashes of Time*.

The story of *Ashes of Time* is set in an identified past when wandering warriors were common, and the sword came to symbolize a preferred way of life and a set of commonly accepted values. However, in the story as depicted in the film, the ethos of this past period comes into an interesting conjunction with the imperatives of an existentialist lifestyle associated with modernity. This conjunction gives a critical energy and a reflective vibrancy to this film which is absent in most other martial arts films. Interestingly, in one of his interviews Wong Kar-wai stated that *Ashes of Time* represents a continuation of *Days of Being Wild*. Hence, although they are set in different time periods, *Ashes of Time* and Wong's other movies share the same mind-set, sensibility and de-validation of desire that permeate his other movies. For characters in this film, as well as those in his other works, contentment is a promise society makes, but rarely keeps. These characters pursue impossible dreams, and it is the psychological and cultural grammar of this impossibility that attracts Wong in constructing his stories. In the final analysis, the director does not offer us final judgments and evaluations but only provisional ones. The ultimate insight of his projected story is that there are no ultimate insights. As a filmmaker who loves to dwell on the interactions between thesis and antithesis, his is a will to catch transitional truths.

The story of *Ashes of Time* is a story of loss. It highlights the experience of loss through numerous visible traces — or as Derrida would say, ashes — that are now a part of the fabric of their daily life. Through these traces, these ashes, the characters in the story aim to recreate the lost world. Hence, the deep sense of nostalgia that is inscribed in the story is a nostalgia for a lost time, and realizing the impossibility of it, it is also a nostalgia for a future moment.

What is interesting about the story of *Ashes of Time* as configured in the film is that it is embedded within another equally fascinating and thought-provoking story. The second story is the story of an innovative filmmaker, infused with a modern sensibility, seeking to clear a cinematic space based on and in violation of the highly codified semiotics of the martial arts form. Both are stories of self-displacement and they mirror and echo each other. In both stories, the production of self-image marks a site of ambivalence charting the turns and returns of subjecthood. The notions of memory, betrayal, search for lost objects, resistance and counter-investments are inscribed equally in both stories. Our gateway to the inscriptions of desire in both stories is memory.

The use of melancholia, as we shall demonstrate in a later chapter, is central to the intent of both narratives. Melancholia marks a site where imagination is transfigured, where self-textualization involves both self-obliteration and self-reinscription, just like for the characters in the film. The filmmaker himself is grappling with melancholia in his effort to make a modernized martial arts film. The melancholia that is shared by the characters in the film is also experienced by the filmmaker. He is caught between the dictates of an established consensual form and the power of a transgressive impulse that yearns for a newness that disowns its newness. In both stories, remembering the past and experiencing the present are both complimentary and adversarial. Here the experience of newness is based on what it denies. The ambiguous existence of the characters in the movie matches that of the filmmaker.

The fantasmatic object of desire — the love object in one story and the sought-for cinematic form in the other — constitutes the driving impulse of both stories. These two objects of desire reflect and hint at each other. Disconnection is an enabling topos in both stories. The characters in the film and the filmmaker are victims of alienated imaginations that are both enabling and disenabling. They are all exiled from their traditional moorings, which creates both fear and excitement in them. In both stories, the illusion of a real world is defeated through fragmentation, juxtapositions of non-congruent temporalities and disparities between aural and visual registers. Both stories are invested in the performative syntax of forgetting and remembering, the ambivalent simultaneity between acceptance and denial and the power of contrary presences. Moreover, in both narratives one has to decode the power of action through its very negation.

As we stated earlier, the idea of betrayal is deeply imprinted in the emotional tribulations of characters in *Ashes of Time* such as Ouyang, Huang, Ouyang's girlfriend, the Sunset Warrior and Murong Yin. Indeed, the filmmaker is also burdened by the knowledge of self-betrayal, the abandoning of a traditionally sanctioned form to displace it with a newer space of enunciation. And we, as viewers of the film who are eternally confined to interpretation, are also burdened by a sense of betrayal in that we seek to impose our own interpretations on the filmic text disregarding the intentions expressed by the filmmaker in numerous interviews and public statements. It is useful to remind ourselves of Nietzsche's characterization of interpreting as, 'forcing, adjudicating, abbreviating, omitting, padding, inventing, falsifying'. Wong's conviction that the filmic text is a site of aporia subtends both the intertwined stories of self-dispossession and self-repossession. Interestingly, the characters in *Ashes of Time* and its maker seek to preserve the past by changing it.

The narrative discourse of *Ashes of Time* can be legitimately described as a castrated discourse. There are many allusions to castration throughout the film. Ouyang abandons the sword in the desert, resolving never to use it again — a mark of castration. The Sunset Warrior is going blind — a signifier of castration as interpreters like Derrida have persuasively argued. Hong Qi lost one of his fingers — another sign of castration. The story deals with a group of characters who are wounded and mutilated by life — yet another reminder of castration that is inscribed in the story.

This stress on castration points to the inability of the characters to take control of their lives and acquire a sense of agency. Indeed they are engaged in a praxis of futility. This is a fear — the uncertainty of acquiring agency — that permeated Hong Kong society in the 1990s, as many were overcome by a sense of powerlessness, a kind of symbolic castration, with reference to Freud. The story of the film may have taken place in a desert some ten or eleven centuries ago, but as we hope to demonstrate in a later chapter, it has a pointed relevance to, and finds echoes in, contemporary anxieties.

4

Characters

The characters in Wong Kar-wai's films are both fascinating and a challenge to the viewer. His characters, and the way he presents them, are different from those in most other Hong Kong films, and it is important to pay close attention to who his characters are and what they say and what they don't say. Within the dialogue the interplay of articulacy and inarticulacy invests Wong Kar-wai's characters with a sense of urgency and self-incomprehension. They seem to be striving for a deeper understanding of their world about which they have very little knowledge. These features are common to characters in most of Wong Kar-wai's films, including *Ashes of Time*.

In this chapter, we wish to focus on six characters in *Ashes of Time* whose destinies are intertwined. None of them, it seems to us, is a fully developed character in the traditional sense with all the complex psychologies animating them laid bare. Indeed, they are presented to us with enigmatic behaviours and half-understood longings. The characters gain definition through their similarities, complimentary qualities and conflicts. The characters traverse each other's space in an elusive manner. They emerge from their shadows only to walk into another shadow.

The central character in *Ashes of Time* is Ouyang Feng. In a sense all others parade before him as they register their anxieties and longings. He is a martial arts swordsman with a difference. At one point in his life he wanted to be a celebrated swordsman in the traditional sense and he had all the skills and resources he needed to achieve this. However, all of this was abandoned when his life took an unexpected turn when his girlfriend rejected him and married his elder brother. This traumatic experience has made him into a man of inaction, tormented by the past and burdened by memory. Instead of fighting for noble and laudable causes and coming to the aid of the helpless, he has become a self-centered cynical mercenary — a death broker. He has become a self-corrupted character who is instrumental in corrupting others. Interestingly, the film's opening images are of Ouyang Feng involved in a fierce sword fight. Clearly, this encounter had taken place some years ago before the current action of the film. It stresses through contrastive imagery what he was then and what he is now. Now, no longer clean-shaven, he has an unkempt appearance and wears a mustache and a beard. He does not fight any more. He has put aside his sword, signifying castration. He has now refashioned himself into a man who gets others to kill for money. Clearly, he is a man who manipulatively preys on the misfortunes of others. At one point he tells Hong Qi in a very matter-of-fact manner, 'Even the best swordsman has to eat and earn a living,' a statement that would hardly come out of the mouth of a typical kung fu movie protagonist. His understanding of reality excludes kindness, generosity and altruism.

Ouyang Feng is also a man given to self-reflection, thereby adding a greater degree of poignancy to his decadence and misery. Interestingly, these ruminations of his also highlight the inconsistencies, contradictions and faults in his thinking. He persuades others to kill for money, saying that it is not a difficult undertaking. At the same time, he tells the audience through his voice-overs that killing is always a difficult enterprise. He has no sense of compassion, generosity or altruism; he comes to the rescue of others only if he is adequately rewarded for his efforts. He is also intolerant of views and actions that contrary to his convictions. For example, when Hong Qi is sick and suffering, he does not come to his aid or fetch a doctor. Instead, he is unhappy with Hong for undertaking a fight with a group of criminals for the price of an egg.

Ouyang Feng is a man overwhelmed by self-imposed misfortunes which impact his life in contradictory ways. He detests the sight of others living in happiness and contentment, as, for example, when he observes Hong Qi and his wife after Hong Qi's recovery from illness. This is, of course, an unconscious and understandable reaction to the misery that he has brought upon himself. Ouyang seems to fancy himself as a thinker with a philosophical cast of mind. In the voice-over narratives, there are several instances of his self-reflective speculations. They are interesting not because of any philosophical depth but rather because they point to his predilection for introspective analysis. These are a few of such examples:

> I used to have the same thought. Seeing a mountain, I'd wonder what lay behind it. But when I crossed it, I found nothing special. Looking back I realized that life there was not so bad.

> Sometimes you don't realize how deeply you are in love with someone until you've separated from each other.

> The harder you try to forget something, the more it'll stick in your memory.

> You would know how to be malicious if you've ever been jealous.

The Zen or Chan Buddhist inspired statement at the commencement of the film, 'The flag is not swaying, nor is the wind blowing. It is the human heart itself that is in tumult,' offers us a useful insight into the mind-set and predicament of Ouyang. What is interesting about this statement is the way in which Wong has changed the original quotation. In the original statement, the operative word is not 'heart' but 'mind'. This is taken from a well-known story in Chan Buddhist scriptures in which Huineng, the sixth patriarch, admonishes two monks who are debating about a flag that was fluttering in the wind. He says that it is neither the flag nor the wind that is fluttering but their own minds. The idea of 'mind' infuses the whole episode with a deep idealism. Wong is reacting against idealism in all his films. Instead, he inserts the word 'heart' which introduces a new trajectory of meaning wholly in keeping with the theme of the film. What this statement, which interfuses the ethos and vision of Zen Buddhism with an existentialist frame of mind, points to the fact that the external world is only a construction of the world of emotions. It underlines the fact that the problems and anguish that beset Ouyang are self-generated. Ouyang, then, presents the image of a kung fu story-protagonist that is totally contrary to the heroes of typical kung fu films. He has only a partial understanding of the dynamics of his inner world, and how it intersects with the outer (to proceed with this binarism) is not of great value to him.

In contrast to Ouyang, Huang Yaoshi, his long-time friend, is a man of the world who is given to sexual adventure. He is someone who is contemptuous and dismissive of social conventions and norms, seeing them as being outmoded and irrelevant. It is interesting that when Huang drinks the amnesiac wine sent to Ouyang by his sister-in-law so that he would be able to forget the past, much of Huang's memory is erased. Interestingly, the only two things he remembers are peach blossoms in spring and a woman by the name of Peach Blossom. He forgets the emotional relations he has had, and fails to keep his appointment with Murong Yang, incurring her fury. He is unable to recall his past camaraderie with the Sunset Warrior — a camaraderie he poisoned by sleeping with his wife. The erasure of his memory results in his aimless itineraries ending his life as a hermit on Peach Blossom Island. Although he likes to see himself as the master of the Peach Blossom Island, he is in fact a hermit, with no contact with the rest of the world and condemned to live an barren and futile life. Although Huang is different from Ouyang, both of them are victims of memory and signify the tragedy of wasted lives. Interestingly, they constantly revisit the past in order to avoid it.

The character of Hong Qi is very different from Ouyang and Huang. In the original novel, of all the five main characters he is the one with the deepest moral convictions. He is a skillful warrior, but is poor and haggard. He goes about on a camel and has no shoes. Ouyang persuades him to fight a gang of horse thieves for money, and Hong begins to subscribe to Ouyang's philosophy of undertaking nothing if there is no financial reward. Ouyang buys him a pair of shoes telling that no one would want to hire 'a shoeless assassin'. The pair of shoes has the intended effect of persuading the harassed villagers to hire him to fight the gang of thieves. He fights valiantly, defeats the gang of thieves and vanquishes the dreaded Left-handed Swordsman. Later, he agrees to come to the aid of a hapless peasant girl with a basket of eggs and avenge the death of her brother by taking on the cruel militiamen. He successfully overpowers and vanquishes them, but in the process he loses one of his fingers. He perceives this as a sign of redemption for his earlier misdeeds of killing for money. Ouyang, on the other hand, sees it differently and is upset with him for killing without adequate financial compensation. After this encounter, the disparities between Ouyang and Hong become evident. Hong tells Ouyang, 'This is me ... I never used to have second thoughts. A strike was a strike. I never gave much thought to values until this girl came to me. I didn't realize I had become so heartless that I could turn her down. I've become another person since I've been around you. I've lost my real self. No, I don't want to be like you.' He resolves to give up the life of killing for money and being of service to others and later becomes the leader of a community of beggars and comes to be known as the Northern Beggar (or Nine-Fingered Mendicant).

The Sunset Warrior, also known as the Blind Swordsman, is another interesting character in the film. He is deeply in love with his wife, and desires his wife's love with equal intensity even as he has serious doubts about his wife's love for him, and even suspects that she is having an affair with one of his friends, Huang Yaoshi. He is filled with a sense of anger and hatred and decides to become a warrior. He is still very much in love with his wife and wishes to see her before he becomes totally blind. To finance his trip back, he agrees to fight for Ouyang. He waits for the gang of horse thieves anxiously. When at last they do come, he fights courageously. However, during the fight he sees in his mind's eye an image of his wife; he is distracted, and consequently killed by the notorious Left-handed Swordsman in the gang. This episode is filmed with great visual imagination. The death of the Sunset Warrior constitutes a significant moment in the film, bringing to the fore some of the important themes that the director is grappling with. The blind swordsman fights valiantly and, at the height of the battle, an image of his wife appears before his eyes. This is indeed the moment when this half-blind swordsman's eyes open and close — he sees his plight and he is killed instantly. Jacques Derrida says that ruin is memory open like an eye. This statement has profound implications for the tragedy of the Sunset Warrior. This is a moment of epiphany in the film when the Sunset Warrior senses through the visage of his wife flashing before his eyes the narcissistic melancholy, the ruin, and his own predicament, in their complex and devastating unity.

The character of Murong Yang/Murong Yin is, in some ways, the most fascinating in the film. After Huang Yaoshi fails to turn up to keep his appointment, and honour his commitment to marry her,

Murong Yin becomes schizophrenic. We are first introduced to her clad in male attire. This is not an uncommon representational strategy in kung fu movies. In her disguise as Yang, she chances to meet the flirtatious Huang, who under the influence of wine says that if Yang had a sister he would marry her. Murong Yin expects him to honour his word. Dressed as a beautiful woman later, Murong Yin awaits him at the agreed time and place. The place is characterized by a tree and a hanging birdcage. But he does not show up. This causes a split in her identity and compels her to act in the way depicted in the film. Wong Kar-wai has dramatized this duality by cleverly juxtaposing images of Murong Yang and Murong Yin.

Ouyang's former girlfriend, who is now his sister-in-law, is an important character in the film in terms of the narrative, although she appears only for a brief period at the end of the film. Wong Kar-wai has said that she is the pivotal character in the film. She was deeply in love with Ouyang, and expected him to profess his love for her. He never did because at that time he was far more interested in excelling in the art of swordsmanship. In sheer anger and desperation, she decides to marry his elder brother. He is never shown in the film. Huang, too, is in love with her. She is fully aware that Ouyang thinks of her most of the time, and hence decides to send the amnesiac wine to him. She thought that once he drinks the wine he would forget the past. Although in the film she is seen only at the very end for a short spell of time, her influence pervades the film diegesis. Her last words to Huang at her death bed take the form of a confession, where she admits her guilt and past errors.

Many of the characters in *Ashes of Time*, whose profiles we have presented briefly, despite their clear differences also share some features in common. They are miserable for having been rejected; they lead solitary lives with very little communication with the rest of the world; they are tormented by the past; there is a complexly entangled relationship among them. We have sought to present this in the form of a diagram (please see appendix 2).

Wong Kar-wai's characters in this film, as well as in his other films, cannot be described as well-rounded and fully developed characters. They are more like fragments of characters than complex totalities. The idea of fragmentation, as we shall show in a later chapter, is central to his ontology, epistemology and aesthetics. The kaleidoscopic presentation of fragments is his approach to reality. We need to construct the characters ourselves on the basis of the fragments presented to us by the film's story. In a sense, the characters are subservient to Wong Kar-wai's larger intellectual pursuit of probing reality that is almost always elusive and ungraspable. In this sense, they are more like pawns in a wider scheme. All moves by the pawns, he seems to be saying, are tentative and provisional. Psychological realism, with all its attendant desiderata, has never been one of Wong Kar-wai's aims. Hence to say, as some critics have, that his characters are not fully developed is to impose a framework that is somewhat alien to Wong Kar-wai's intentions.

Wong Kar-wai's mode of characterization is intimately related to his narrative structure and visual poetics. The images that he projects on the screen have a way of undermining their own authority and stability of meaning as they are often recontextualized within newer regimes of significance. Moreover, his self-conscious juxtapositions of aural and visual signifiers have the effect of creating a fissured textual surface complicating the easy understanding of characters. Reconstructing the narrative and reconstructing the characters is part of the job of the viewer in a Wong Kar-wai film.

Most of the characters in *Ashes of Time*, as in his other films spend their days in fear of rejection or seeking to overcome rejection. This comes across in Ouyang's narrations although he is not rejected in the strict sense of the term, he talks about himself as if he has been totally abandoned. Murong Yin, as a consequence of her being rejected by Huang, creates an elder brother for herself.

The Sunset Warrior is a man who is rejected by his wife, and although he is deeply in love with her, the only real issue confronting him is self-annihilation. Huang loves Ouyang's sister-in-law, but she is in love with Ouyang. As Ouyang is mortally scared of being rejected, he cannot bring himself to declare his love for her. The only two characters in the film who are unafraid of being rejected, and therefore who acquire a sense of self-confidence and emotional equilibrium, are Hong Qi and the peasant girl. They are so successful in overcoming this fear that has paralyzed the other characters that in the concluding images of the film we see their influence on Ouyang's decision to leave the desert. As Wong Kar-wai himself has stated, the fear of rejection is a theme that runs through all his movies. This results in the continual depiction of a curious and agonistic fantasy of self-presence.

When we discuss characterization in a novel or a film, we invariably refer to, or bring within the perimeter of discussion, the question of identity. Each character's identity is of crucial importance. However, in *Ashes of Time* the identities of characters flow in and out of each other. Wong Kar-wai seems to deconstruct identity only to bring out its further complexities. The idea of doubling and splitting figure very prominently in *Ashes of Time*. Murong Yang/Murong Yin is the most obvious example. However there are other doublings and splittings as, for example, between Ouyang and Huang, who, though different, are also complimentary. Rene Girard is of the view that twins are usually considered a threat in view of the fact that their physical similarity underlines the dissolution of difference that is so feared in primitive societies.[1] To make things even more complicated, there are doublings and splittings across films, as such the characters that Leslie Cheung plays in *Days of Being Wild* and *Ashes of Time* have many similarities. Hence the simple equation between characters and self-enclosed and transparent identities that many filmmakers seem to emphasize does not figure very prominently in Wong Kar-wai's film poetics.

In order to understand the way in which Wong Kar-wai seeks to give a figurative quality to his characters, one has to pay particular attention to the question of time. For the characters in *Ashes of Time*, the present is a mere shadow of the past. The constant repetitions serve to underline this fact; the intimacies of the characters are lost in time, and memories can hardly bring them back to life. The slow motions, fast motions and freeze-frame cinematography bring out through visual significations the tragic engagement of the characters with time. We will discuss Wong Kar-wai's philosophy of time in a subsequent chapter.

An examination of the ways in which Wong presents his characters on the screen points out the misleading generalizations associated with the suture theory. Suture theory maintains that films entice audiences into ready identification with characters, resulting in ideological play. The film constitutes an imaginary signifier that has the effect of persuading the viewer to identify with the characters and thereby investing him or her with an identity that is reflective of the dominant ideological discourse of the given culture. However, a film like *Ashes of Time* points out the simplistic nature of this assumption. Suture theory is based on the notion of passive participation of a universal viewer and the easy identification with characters on screen. In the case of *Ashes of Time*, neither is true. Wong does not promote such facile identifications. In point of fact, he strives to secure a critical distance between the viewers and the characters. Furthermore, in order to understand the nature and significance of his characters, far from being a passive participant, the viewer has to be critically engaged with the film diegesis.

There is a certain poetry in the characterization in *Ashes of Time*. This might appear to be a strange statement. The poetry of the visuals, ably supported by Christopher Doyle, is of course evident throughout the film. However, there is a kind of poetry in the very conceptualization of characters. Roland Barthes once remarked that the opposite of poetry is not prose but stereotypes. The characters in *Ashes of Time* are not stereotypes. Using the kung fu genre as a counterfoil, Wong creates his characters through the disavowal of the anticipated and challenges to stereotypes. In Jean-Luc Godard's *Pierrot le fou*, there is a statement to the effect that poetry grows out of ruins. Many of the characters in this film are amidst ruins or experiencing the force of ruin. Their uniqueness emerges from the debris of their life, generating a sense of poetry in the Godardian sense. Paul Valery once compared prose and verse to walking and dancing, respectively. Prose has a clear end in view and is largely guided teleologically. It proceeds directly towards its end. In the case of verse, which is like dancing, there is constant digression, encircling, repetition and it is not guided teleologically. When we examine the behaviour of the characters in *Ashes of Time*, we realize that they dance rather than walk, although often it is not physically but mentally.

Raymond Williams, in his writings on theatre and film, employed the term 'complex seeing' to designate the power of diagnostic understanding that serves to deepen or validate the experiences presented through them. We could purposefully extend this idea of complex seeing to fathom the interactions and inter-subjectivities among characters in a film as well. Moreover, in a film or stage drama, complex seeing implies complex hearing, and this has deep ramifications for the meaning inscribed in *Ashes of Time*. Many of the characters in the firm are motivated by the power of absent speech, the unuttered and desperately sought-for statement. Despite the visual density and richness, it is the unfilled aural space that is at the center of the narrative discourse. Ouyang wishes to hear the word 'yes' to his suggestion of elopement. His girlfriend was yearning to hear 'I love you' coming from his lips. Murong Yang/Yin is pining to hear words to the effect that Huang will marry his sister/herself. The Sunset Warrior would like nothing more than to hear words of reciprocal love from his wife. Hence the resonance of the unspoken word pervades the narrative of *Ashes of Time*, making the ear the privileged sensory organ for each of the characters mentioned above. Indeed, paradoxically, the exuberant visuals of the film create an inviting sight for hearing. These characters are activated by the reconstructed slogan, 'hearing is believing'. Consequently they are victims of both underhearing and overhearing.

Despite the vibrancy of the visual images, it is the echo, the sound and the word that the characters are after. It is the hearing eye that propels the story, calling to mind Shakespeare's injunction in King Lear, 'Look with thine ears.' And a character in *Happy Together* says, 'You can see much better with your ears.' We repeatedly perceive in the film how the characters look disconsolately out of the images projected onto the screen, straining to hear the unspoken words. They experience those words negatively as a terrifying absence. Standing amidst the sepulchral wreckage of their lives, Ouyang Feng, Huang Yaoshi, Ouyang's girlfriend, the Sunset Warrior and Murong Yang/Yin value the ear over the eye as the primary sensory organ. This reminds us of Derrida's statement: 'The ear is uncanny; uncanny is what it is; double is what it can become.'² Instead of the Buddhist idea of the third eye being eye of insight, the fantastic space of desire in *Ashes of Time* is guarded by the third ear.

5

Narrative Structure

Wong Kar-wai is not a popular filmmaker in the way that, say, John Woo is. Many of his films have failed to generate widespread audience interest. His *Ashes of Time*, which was billed as a martial arts movie based on the popular work of Jin Yong, was eagerly awaited by the local audiences, but when it was first shown, many found it to be a let-down, hardly living up to expectations. For example, there were very few battle scenes and action sequences with the flying and bounding swordsmen that audiences had come to expect of martial arts movies. Part of the reason for audiences' disappointment and disenchantment with Wong Kar-wai's films resides in his narrative structure. It is one that is highly convoluted and demands close critical attention to the sequences unfolding before the viewers. Indeed, most of Wong Kar-wai's films, with the possible exception of his latest two films, *Happy Together* and *In the Mood for Love*, do not contain narrative structures that are easy to follow and respond to. It is on account of this fact that many consider his films to be 'difficult', 'confusing' and 'disorganized'. Some even go to the extent of branding him a 'pretentious' filmmaker.

In order to understand the ontological and aesthetic significance of Wong Kar-wai's cinematic creations, we need to pay close attention to the concept of narrative structure. For him, narrative in cinema is not a mere continuous and unbroken unfolding of events in time, a transparent act of communication, as is the case with most films. His intention is to present the narrative in self-contained and complexly connected chains of signification that are arranged in terms of the imperatives of psychological and epistemological time rather than chronological time. Hence, the complex imbrications of past, present and future. Moreover, in staging his narrative Wong Kar-wai seems to underline the importance of deploying all the resources of cinema as elements in the narrative. The actors, editing, sound, silences, light and shade are all constitutive elements of the narrative discourse. These elements have a way of drawing attention to themselves that further erode the notion of a simple, linear and continuous narrative. How images speak, don't speak, and at times misspeak is all part of the narrative of *Ashes of Time*. What happens between and beyond self-enclosed sequences is as important as what transpires within them. When seen in this light, one begins to appreciate the complex density and syntactical convolutions in his narrative structures.

The fragmentation, discontinuities and complex intermixing of time frames give the narrative of *Ashes of Time* its density and convoluted appearance. The narrative discourse of the film, in essence, consists of four main segments. The first is the relationship between Ouyang Feng and Huang Yaoshi. The second is the relationship between Ouyang and the Sunset Warrior. The third segment comprises the interaction between Ouyang and Murong Yin/Yang, and the fourth is between Ouyang and Hong Qi. All the characters, then, parade before the protagonist, Ouyang Feng, who is the pivot around which they revolve. Additionally, Ouyang's former girlfriend, who appears briefly at the end of the film, is a continuing absence felt throughout the story. These four relationships constitute the bulk of the story. There are indeed interesting commonalities, reciprocities, and common interests among these characters. Each becomes a part of the other's life in complex ways, investing the narrative with a multifaceted quality. Ouyang and Huang are both in love with Ouyang's former girlfriend. Huang and the Sunset Warrior are linked by the fact that the latter is deeply in love with his wife and his wife is deeply in love with Huang, and, at the same time, the Sunset Warrior works for Ouyang. Murong Yin is in love with Huang, and Murong Yin and Murong Yang each expect contradictory actions from Ouyang. The peasant girl, who is not related in any way to the characters so far mentioned, serves to precipitate a complex relationship between Ouyang and Hong Qi. The relationships are complicated and the way that Wong Kar-wai has chosen to tell their stories, by defying standard narrative techniques and complicating the time frames, adds to the difficulty of some viewers in following the story.

What makes the narrative structure in *Ashes of Time* so complicated is the fact that these relationships are not dramatized sequentially and in a linear fashion. The narrative segments intersect each other in a complex rhythm. Moreover, there are numerous flashbacks, flashbacks within flashbacks, shifts of viewpoint, dislocations and elisions that have the effect of creating a fractured textual surface. This narrative complexity is further compounded by the frequent use of voice-over monologues that serve to both to clarify, at times to lend irony, undermine and confound the authority of the narrative. Indeed, this has become a kind of trademark of Wong Kar-wai's narrative structure and is clearly evident in his other films as well.

Memory, with its complicated and ambiguous relationship to time, plays a crucial role in the narrative, inflecting it in unforeseen ways. The English title of the film, with its emphasis of the march of time, its destructibility and resurrection in memory, signifies this fact. In Wong's films, memory has a way of inflecting everyday life, history, experience and desire, and connecting them to new terrains of cognition. 'Being in the world' for him is 'being in memory'. In *Ashes of Time* as well as in his other films, reality is not objective or mind-independent, but a subjective construction based on memory and desire. If memory is both a retrieval and obfuscation of the past, and desire is the straining towards the unrealizable in the Lacanian sense, the superimposition of memory on desire, and desire on memory result in unpredictable eruptions. This is another reason for the obscurity that some associate with his narrative structure. In addition, his prioritizing of representation over mimesis, and of visible linkages over invisible flows, adds depth and complexity to his narrative structure.

There are a number of other aspects that we need to focus on as we seek to unravel the opaque and complicated narrative structure of *Ashes of Time*. These relate to issues of culturally sanctioned topoi, intertextuality and the constitutive interplay between being and role-playing. One can identify several important culturally sanctioned topoi that are inscribed in the filmic text. We wish to focus on three of them. The first is the topos of the sword. It is hardly surprising that the topos of the sword figures so prominently in the narrative discourse of *Ashes of Time*, being a martial arts film. In the world of Chinese martial arts, weapons come to epitomize the social status and subjectivity of their owners. In terms of the hierarchy of categorization, the sword is the most prestigious, influential and valued of the weapons. The sword invests the owner with a sense of superiority. Ouyang, Huang and the Sunset Warrior possess swords. In contrast, Hong Qi does not have a sword. He is a poor, barefooted warrior of inferior standing. However, as the narrative unfolds, it is Hong Qi, with his inferior weapon, who emerges as the morally admirable warrior of the four, thereby undercutting the cherished hierarchies and symbolism associated with martial arts films.

The peach blossom is another interesting topos that underlies the narrative of the film. Ouyang, Huang and the Sunset Warrior share a common interest in the peach blossom. According to the culturally-grounded associations, peach blossoms represent the highly glorified and idealized realm of sophisticated ambition and desire. They indicate an unreal world of desire. They also have come to symbolize the unattainable, evanescent, pure and unforgettable. The common desire of all three characters has a vital connection with the topos of the peach blossoms. It animates the narrative in an intriguingly subtle manner.

The third topos that we wish to focus on is the mountain and what is beyond it. This topos carries with it a sense of mystery and unknown destiny. Ouyang's recurrent question as to what is beyond the mountain is reflective of this frame of mind. Ouyang muses that whenever he saw the mountain it aroused a sense of the beyond with its curiosities and unknowns. However, at the end of the film the power of this topos is also subverted by Ouyang's realization that there is nothing of consequence beyond and his patent lack of interest in it. What is interesting about these topoi is that they underlie the narrative structure and invest it with the cultural optic which of course takes the narrative to a different plane. This has the effect of complicating what is already a complicated narrative structure. There is a fusion of the narrative horizon with a cultural horizon that results in a multivalent narrative discourse.

The isolation, solitude, lack of communication and obfuscations that characterize the lives of the protagonists in *Ashes of Time* are not merely narrated through the events but are enacted in them. The structuring of the events gives definition to those events. In other words, the displacements, discontinuities, ellipses and fragmentations that distinguish the narrative structure are reflective and emblematic of the predicament of the leading characters. To phrase it differently, the diegesis and performativity mutually reinforce each other.

Wong Kar-wai is not a naive realist; he incorporates aspects of the fantastic as a way of deepening our sense of realism. The hypnotic quality that pervades the film is as much a product of the visual imagination as it is of the narrative architecture. According to Todorov, the fantastic marks a point of hesitation and indecision, caught as we are between the uncanny and the marvelous and what is cognitively acceptable and what is not. *Ashes of Time* is a prolongation of that moment of hesitation into a cast of mind and an inescapable part of reality. The narrative structure with its affirmations as well as negations of reality, contribute to the achievement of this effect. This has the effect of highlighting the inadequacies and limitations of simple, linear narratives that we have come to expect of films calculated to entertain us. Instead of uncomplicated and comforting enjoyment, Wong Kar-wai is after complex and demanding pleasures. Both are, of course, aspects of cinematic entertainment. The characters in *Ashes of Time* daydream, hallucinate, ponder and reflect and all these activities are an integral part of the stories that they intend to tell. These narratives are addressed to others, to themselves and, at times, to the audience directly and intimately. It is the intention of the director to eliminate any ontological demarcations among these diverse forms of address. The quality of the fantastic that we alluded to earlier and the dream-like quality are reinforced by this narrative structure.

As we have mentioned throughout this chapter the narrative structure of *Ashes of Time* is demanding and is not one that promotes relaxed participation. As a film director, Wong discourages complacent readings of his works. The viewer has to be active to the point of being a co-creator of meaning. Although the textual surface is fissured, fragmented and opaque, he also provides a road map if you are willing to look for it in the clues and hints he has planted. For example, the self-projections and self-readings of Ouyang are a vital part of the experience of the film and its narrative organization. The female characters of the story bring to his mind the image of his sister-in-law with whom he is still deeply in love despite his attempts at suppression, sublimation and denial. Similarly, he perceives in the characters of Huang Yaoshi and the Sunset Warrior reflections of his own selfhood. Reflections are, of course, a deeply embedded visual trope in *Ashes of Time*. Such self-projections and self-readings that add clarity to the narrative and the motivations of characters require close reading of the text. The average filmgoer is often not prepared to undertake such narrative reconstructions.

The idea of narrative logic is vital to an understanding of the narrative structure of a given film. In most films, most often the narrative logic is transparent and self-evident. The motivations are clear; the causal links between events are cogent; the flow of time is intelligible. There is a sense of predictability in the way the events unfold. In the case of *Ashes of Time* that narrative logic is not apparent and demands the active participation of the viewer. The two main ingredients of narrative are story and plot. The story provides us with a sequence of events over time and the textual information needed to see them in a context, while the plot provides the element of causality answering the questions of why and where for. In the case of *Ashes of Time* the story line is unclear just as much as the plot line, thereby making a great demands on the viewer. To understand the narrative logic informing the narrative structure is to go a long way in grasping the narrative structure. As Stokes and Hoover[1] have pointed out,

> Critics describe the metaphysical and existential nature of Wong's films, touching on Sartrean philosophy in which individuals are defined by their actions. Characters are simply there, without reason, whether 'there' is an unidentifiable desert or contemporary urban Hong Kong. Characterization seems motivated by futile passions, lives constantly trying to escape from themselves, acts fated to be incomplete.

A proper understanding of the narrative logic would help in erasing some of these undeniable difficulties.

The topic of memory is central to the meaning of *Ashes of Time* and it has an important bearing on the narrative structure. How memory shapes, distorts, makes, unmakes, enriches and diminishes the past cannot be separated from the narrative discourse. Whether memory preserves the past or distorts it is a question that cannot be ignored when considering the narrative organization of the film. Bergson was of the opinion that we spatialize the past, particularly if we are inclined to focus on a specific moment from the past.[2] This spatialization is evident throughout the film and is closely linked to the impulses behind the narrative structure. Much of the meaning of the characters like Ouyang, his girlfriend, Murong Yang and the Sunset Warrior resides in these selective reconstructions of the past. Consequently, they can be said to be the sum of their memory. We stated that Wong Kar-wai tends to spatialize the past. This is connected not only to his use of memory of the various characters but also to his desire for analysis — analysis is a way of spatialization where you display the various incidents side by side in a cartographic gesture. By his own admission, when writing the script for this film, Wong was influenced by the two celebrated Latin American writers, Garcia Marquez and Manuel Puig. Interestingly, they also favour complex narrative structures with discontinuities and fragmentations and spatializations of memory.

As we stated earlier, the intention of Wong Kar-wai was to make a martial arts film with a difference, a *wuxia* film with a postmodernist visage. This meant, of course, working within and against and upon the layered tradition of the martial arts genre. To be sure, Wong Kar-wai was not the only *wuxia* film director who sought to experiment with the form. King Hu and Zhang Che in the 1960s and 70s and Tsui Hark and Ching Siu-tung in the 90s made very significant efforts in this direction. *Once Upon a Time in China I* and *II* directed by Tsui Hark, and the *Swordsman* series, also produced by Tsui Hark, are extremely important in this regard. We will have more to say on this aspect in chapter 7, 'Martial Arts'. In the case of Wong, he went beyond the transforming desire to deconstruct the genre and to interrogate its viability as an art form with a contemporary viewpoint. This aim is clearly reflected in his style, as we hope to demonstrate in the next chapter. But this aim manifests itself in the convolutions and disjunctures in the narrative structure as well. The dominant features of *Ashes of Time* that we have discussed so far have had the effect of displacing the mode of narration of this *wuxia* film into a different realm of representation and a different level of articulation.

It is evident that Wong Kar-wai has constructed his narrative in a self-interrogatory mode, inviting the viewers to connect and disconnect, include and exclude, and emphasize and ignore certain events and incidents that constitute the narrative chain and to identify intersections in the diverse narrative trajectories. Viewers must also differentiate between various narrative levels and mediate discrepant registers of space and time. Wong wishes to make the spectator of the film into a quintessentially late twentieth-century subject, overwhelmed by confusions, dead-ends, fragmentations, illusions of coherence, and constitutive uncertainties. The overall effect of the complex narrative structure is to make it an analogue, or a discursive correlate, of late twentieth-century anxieties. The narrative structure invites the spectator to be a co-creator of meaning, piecing together the action and its significance, thereby transferring to him or her, to an appreciable extent, the narrative authority of the text. The play of possibility, which is intrinsic to the narrative designs of *Ashes of Time*, as well as its betrayals of hesitancy make the co-creative role of the spectator that much more important. When we analyse the narrative structure of this film, we are left with the feeling that the sense of agency has been passed on to the spectators by the characters as well as by the narrators of the story.

Another reason why some viewers flounder and fumble when faced by the narrative structure of the film is that it presupposes the operation of narrative codes that are not part of the mental furniture of the average martial arts movie fan. Roland Barthes, in discussing the nature and significance of narrative, proposed five codes: an action code, a hermeneutic code, a semic code, a symbolic code and a cultural code. The functions of the codes, according to Barthes, is to make the narrative world into one which is familiar to each viewer, because he or she will have been there before. The action code deals with the actions in a narrative as well as the reasons for undertaking them, which are almost always known beforehand. The hermeneutic code refers to the riddles to be solved and secrets to be uncovered in a narrative. The semic code is also designated by the term connotative code. Its function is to facilitate the task of the reader or the viewer in piecing together various aspects of the content and to direct our attention to how they enable the deepening of our understanding of the dramatis personae in the narrative. The symbolic code works to uncover and explain certain concepts and motifs that inform the narrative. Finally, the cultural code serves to direct the attention of the viewer to the cultural thought-world on which the narrative is constructed. Cultural presuppositions figure significantly in this code. What is interesting about the narrative of *Ashes of Time* is that it complicates all five codes and makes the task of the viewer that much more arduous and demanding. Let us consider, for example, the symbolic code in a typical martial arts film and that of *Ashes of Time*. In a typical martial arts film, the symbolic code works, for example, by focusing on the binarism between good and evil, moral and immoral. The protagonists are almost always good, moral and valiant. This is certainly not the case in *Ashes of Time* where the characters are a mix of good and evil and without any sense of moral heroism. In the case of the average martial arts film, it presupposes a cultural world of heroism, morality and patriotism that is familiar to the audiences. No such familiar cultural thought-world exists in Wong's film. Hence the way he deploys the various narrative codes also adds to the difficulties certain viewers encounter with the narrative structure of the film.

6

Style

Wong Kar-wai is widely believed to be a disorganized filmmaker who has a tendency to improvise on the set without much pre-planning and forethought. This impression has been created partly by newspaper accounts that describe his approach to filmmaking. It has also been strengthened by superficial examinations of the narrative structures and stylistic devices in his films. Despite appearances, he is a careful and meticulous film director whose work displays a compelling inner organization and a fidelity to his personal cinematic grammar. His filmic style, conjunctions and disjunctions of word and image, visual rhetoric and representational strategies bear the mark of a filmmaker who is dedicated to the mastery of his craft.

The style of *Ashes of Time* is integral to the meaning of the film. Indeed, the style is the meaning of the film. Normally there is a widespread tendency to regard style as a formal element that imparts a visual beauty to the narrative. Style is often explained in terms of conformity to the accepted syntax of cinema. However, for Wong Kar-wai, style signifies something deeper and central to the very being of his film. For him, style is a vital mode of thinking and a part of his epistemology. His epistemology is realized through compositions, framing, camera angles, editing, lighting and the use of sound and music. Images produced by the camera and the flow of images modulated by editing — sometimes smooth and sometimes jumpy — underpin this style.

Ashes of Time has all the characteristics we have now come to associate with the work of Wong Kar-wai. Viewers familiar with his earlier films such as *As Tears Go By* and *Days of Being Wild* will immediately see his stylistic signature. The jump-cuts, slow motion sequences, freeze frames, unusual camera angles and voice-overs are part of his repertoire of representational strategies. For example, throughout *Ashes of Time* we see vast, empty and brilliantly radiant sands of the desert, the changing visage of the sky, rolling waves of the sea and tranquil waters reflecting the shadows of lonely characters. Wong doesn't use this natural scenery to symbolize the mental outlook and dispositions of characters or to add a further element of picturesqueness to the narrative, as most filmmakers might do. His intention, rather, is to delineate the disjunction between the characters and their milieu. There is a disparity between the vast open landscapes and the cramped and constrictive lives of the characters.

Ashes of Time, being a martial arts movie, has numerous scenes that bring swordplay into the narrative and spectacle in interesting ways. However, the way the director has chosen to present them visually is different from run-of-the-mill martial arts movies. Rather than focus on full-body action shots or close-ups on faces and acrobatics in brilliant light, he focuses on shadowy figures partially seen through a haze as fragmented bodies in an encompassing thickness. Two of the crucial battles scenes are those between the Sunset Warrior (Blind Swordsman) fighting the gang of horse thieves and Hong Qi fighting the same gang. We see Wong Kar-wai's stylistic propensities clearly in evidence in these sequences.

Let us consider the battle between the Sunset Warrior and the gang of horse thieves, and how the director has elected to present it visually. We see a series of loosely linked shots — slow motion, fast motion, jump-cuts and darkened visuals — that serve to undermine the continuity and cohesion of the episode. The slow motion camerawork has the carefully planned effect of unsettling the accepted norms of space and time. As Ackbar Abbas has pointed out, the fight between the Blind Swordsman and the gang of thieves is a fight against light.[1] In most sequences dealing with swordplay, human figures can only be distinguished one from another when the sequence is shot in slow-motion and has enough light. *Ashes of Time* reminds us of the uncertain actions of characters trapped in prisons of their own making.

At times, Wong Kar-wai has an interesting way of visually literalizing verbal metaphors that adds a fascinating dimension to his repertoire of representational strategies. Ouyang Feng says that Murong Yin is fighting her own reflection. Throughout the film there are sequences that focus on Murong Yin's shadows, reflections of her figure in water, and the memorably portrayed love scene in which Ouyang Feng, Huang Yaoshi, Murong Yin, and Ouyang Feng's former lover are involved in vivid superimpositions of images dictated by memory. There are, of course, many such examples of verbal metaphors being literalized through visual images. Towards the end of the film, a candle drops into the thickening darkness signifying the ending of a relationship.

Despite the interconnections and interactions among the various characters in the film, there are also dislocations and disjunctures among them. Interestingly, each of the characters enters into the personal space of the other characters only to realize how distant each is from the others. Wong Kar-wai's visual style seems to reinforce this point in compelling and complex ways. For example, the closing shots of the film provide us with a montage of diverse scenes focusing on the self-imprisonment of the main characters in their self-created and insular worlds. Once again we see how the director of *Ashes of Time* has deployed his filmic imagination and stylistic predilections as a way of thinking and an epistemological strategy.

As we stated earlier, the way images are constructed and the way they function in propelling and giving shape to the narrative discourse merits close study. This is indeed a vital function performed by filmic style. *Ashes of Time* deals with memory: the main characters are guided, wounded, exhilarated and overwhelmed by it and, at the same time, resentful of it. Although individual memory is private, the specularization of it has to be public. It is here that the role of the image, as Wong Kar-wai understands it, becomes crucially important. Here we wish to invoke the theories of two outstanding film theorists. The first is the Italian poet, film director and thinker Pier Paolo Pasolini. He talks about the 'brute' nature, physicality and palpability of images which can revise our original perceptions of the world in new ways. Cinematic images are like memories and dreams. The oneiric quality that pervades *Ashes of Time* is a consequence of the powerful use of cinematic images by the director. Pasolini remarks that 'images come to form a reality' in which objects are 'charged with meaning and utter a brute speech by their very presence'. This brute speech, according to Pasoloni, is pre-linguistic and shows the unconscious preoccupations of a given community.[2] This approach to image and cinema should throw valuable light on the ambitions of Wong Kar-wai in *Ashes of Time*. For example, in the scene in which Peach Blossom caresses the horse, the way it is shot and the use of light and shade create a sense of repressed eroticism that highlights the power of images that Pasolini is talking about.

The second theorist that we wish to invoke is the French philosopher Gilles Deleuze. His notions of *movement-image* and *time-image* are extremely significant in this regard. Movement-images, which are the common coin in most films, serve to structure the events of the story in a sequential and orderly manner. Time-images, which came into existence with self-reflective modern cinema, have a way of going beyond the ordering of events to provoke a critical thinking by a process of distantiation. Time-images, according to Deleuze, are a way of reading cinema that is decidedly critical and self-reflexive. He remarks that time-image is a way of 'thinking in cinema through cinema'.[3] This line of inquiry connects very nicely with the intentions of Wong Kar-wai as he seeks to provoke us into critical thought and self-reflexivity through his images. Let us, as an example, consider the following episode. Towards the end of the film, Ouyang Feng's former girlfriend and now sister-in-law, is shown framed by a window. She is wearing extremely bright and boldly coloured clothes, signifying a moment of happiness. She gazes at the ocean, and also at her child who plays nearby. The way she is framed, the colourful clothes she wears and the child who is playing add up to a picture of hope, happiness and contentment. However, we also realize that she is a victim of her own making, battling the errors of a cruel fate, just like Ouyang Feng. What is interesting to note here is that the focus is not on the superficial appearance of the character but the underside of her emotionality. It is this moment of meditation that provokes a sense of critical thinking and self-reflexivity on the part of the audience.

One of the stylistic trademarks of Wong Kar-wai is his marvelous ability to create spatial fluidity. He ingeniously uses camerawork for this purpose, adding to the totality of impact through his framing, lighting, quick cutting, articulations and non-articulations within and between shots. The bold use of lighting, focus, speed and filters in the film leaves us with the impression that the director and cinematographer are in perfect unison exploiting all the available resources to generate a sense of spatial fluidity. This aspect of Wong's style is clearly in evidence in *Ashes of Time* as well. Esther Yau has made the observation that Wong

Kar-wai and his hugely talented cameraman, Christopher Doyle, have 'collaboratively assembled a different kind of cinematic visuality — one in which seductive images, erotic sensations, and electronic music combine to subtend the repeated motifs of loneliness, longing and memory.'[4]

Another stylistic device in *Ashes of Time* that merits close attention is the imaginative use of voice-overs as both a means of establishing intimacy and distance, and reinforcing and undermining the authority of the images. It is also a means of supplying us with information that the narrative does not make available to us, reinforcing the loneliness of characters and inviting us into their private fantasies. This is a representational strategy that Wong Kar-wai has used with remarkable skill in many of his other films as well. The voice-over narrations are by turns philosophical, ruminative, witty, self-reflexive and poetical. They can be both coherent and disjointed and induce a dream-like effect that is perfectly in keeping with the ethos that pervades the film. Moreover, at times, the voice-overs perform a destabilizing function by creating a disjunction between the content of the voice-over and the testimony of the images. This tension serves to strengthen the decentering ambitions of the filmmaker.

The visual style of *Ashes of Time*, like its narrative structure, is complex and unsettling. Let us, for example, consider the opening images of the film when Ouyang Feng and Huang Yaoshi are introduced to us. The visuals are powerful but do not quite coalesce. The sudden dislocations of space and time, bold camera angles, stop action, jump cuts and the chiaroscuro effects serve to introduce a sense of fracturedness and dislocation that is at the heart of the experience of the film. Here the ambiguities of the style enact the thematics of the film. Moreover, the camera plays a crucial role in the narrative discourse, much in the manner of a character in the film. For example, in *Ashes of Time*, the camera surveys the expansive loneliness of locations while contributing to it.

When examining the style of Wong Kar-wai, as manifest in *Ashes of Time*, we have to pay attention not only to the visualities and the specularizations but also to the use of music and sound. Indeed, music is as important as the images in the construction of meaning in his films. In many of his films popular songs play a central role in the thematic articulation, such as, the song 'California Dreamin'', in *Chungking Express*. The song memorably captures the hopes and aspirations of Faye. The following comment by Wong Kar-wai illustrates the functionality of music in his films:[5]

> As part of our life, music has become an indication telling us where and when we are. In my own films, I try to figure out what kind of environment that is, including its geographical area, and what kind of noise this place would have. What kind of smell? What are the identities of the people in this environment? What do they do there? But sometimes I start with music in mind. This is hard to explain. My instinct is that film must have a kind of atmosphere that matches a certain period. In *Chungking Express*, for instance, I knew from the beginning that it must be 'California Dreamin'' — innocent, and simple, like summertime in the 1970s. During the planning stage, I did not have a script. When Chris Doyle, my cinematographer, asked me what this film was about, I played 'California Dreamin'' to him.

This statement by Wong Kar-wai gives us a clear sense of the centrality of music in his films. In most of his films, a song not only serves to create a mood but also aids in the progression of the narrative and encapsulates the theme of the film. Whether in *Happy Together* or *Chungking Express* this becomes evident. In *Ashes of Time*, we find a combination of a range of music styles. What is interesting about *Ashes of Time* is that although it is a period film set in an unidentified period in the past, the sensibility inscribed in the filmic text is one of modernism and even postmodernism. Hence, rather than confining himself to classical Chinese music, he has sought to make use of a international music that is in keeping with the international sensibility of the film.

The way Wong Kar-wai uses music in his films in an interesting way that differs considerably from most Hong Kong filmmakers. He does not employ music to signify a social context or physical environment, nor is it a metonym of the immediate physical arena of action. Instead, he uses music to draw our attention to a world of interiority, a fantasy world that the characters both seek refuge in and strive to escape from. Through music he attempts to give expression to the unarticulated emotions of characters. The discrepancy between the immediate environment of action and the music is clearly seen in films such as *Days of Being Wild*, which takes place in the 60s, but uses music that was popular in the late 40s.

In *Ashes of Time*, which operates through the framework of a martial arts film, one would expect to find Chinese music used liberally. Instead, what we find is a musical score that has been influenced by Ennio Morricone's music that he wrote for spaghetti Westerns. Interestingly, this is despite the fact that the director of music of *Ashes of Time*, Frankie Chan, was formerly a martial arts choreographer. The relationship between characters and music in Wong Kar-wai's films is complex and multifaceted. Music seems to create the characters' fantasy worlds as well as to destabilize them and strengthen the narrative as well as to disrupt it. In other words, music for Wong is a stratagem of connection as well as disconnection. Although music does not figure as centrally in *Ashes of Time* as it does in some of his other films such as *Days of Being Wild*, *Chungking Express* and *Happy Together*, it is evident that the kind of hybrid music that he employs in *Ashes of Time* and the way he employs it deserves careful attention.

Wong Kar-wai, in this film, as in his other works, seems to be playing with space and time. This is a characteristic feature of his cinematic style. He has an interesting way of interweaving episodes in which different characters and different situations are reconfigured. Moreover, one comes across instances of the playful treatment of time within a single scene. For instance, in the scene in which Huang Yaoshi confides to Murong Yin (disguised as Yang) that if she had a sister he would marry her, Murong Yin drops a chopstick. Then we are shown her picking it up. However, what is interesting is that this shot leads to the next shot in which we see the chopstick falling to the ground. This kind of play with time and space, the inversion of tense, becomes a part of his visual grammar. Similarly, the contradictions in the identification of time found in Ouyang Feng's diary-like narration also point in this direction.

Such instances of dislocation and disjointedness draw our attention to what Gilles Deleuze would term 'falsifying narrative'. Wong Kar-wai uses irony and falsifying narrative to undercut the authority of the narration and representation of the film. Contradictions between the voice-overs and images, inverted tenses and plays on spatialities and temporalities contribute to this undermining of authority. This ties in which his decentering and anti-hierarchical impulses. As we stated earlier, style for Wong Kar-wai is a mode of thinking, an epistemological excursion. The world in Wong's movies is fragmented, incoherent and full of dislocations, fissures and discrepancies. To make sense of such a world, he seems to be arguing that we need a visual style that is complex, playful, serious, self-reflexive, unorthodox, innovative and that is capable of grasping unseen realities. He is moving towards such an ideal. In order to understand the true dimensions of Wong Kar-wai's endeavour, we have to see how his camera follows its own instincts, irrespective of the demands of the narrative, and how powerful and memorable images without a narrative anchor have a way of guiding our visual and cognitive interests.

Let us amplify this point a little further. Michel Foucault in his book, *The Order of Things,* refers to a passage in Borges which quotes a 'certain Chinese encyclopedia' in which it is written that, 'animals are divided into, (a) belonging to the emperor, (b) embalmed, (c) tame, (d) sucking eggs, (e) sirens, (f) fabulous, (g) stray dogs, (h) included in the present classification, (i) frenzied, (j) innumerable, (k) drawn with a very fine camelhair brush, (l) et cetera, (m) having just broken the water pitcher, (n) that from a long way off look like flies.' Foucault believes that this passage violates 'all the familiar landmarks of my thought ... breaking up all the planes with which we are accustomed to tame the wild profusion of existing things.'[6] What this categorization dramatizes is the arbitrary ways in which we categorize the world. Wong Kar-wai believes that the normal ways in which we categorize the world are as arbitrary as any other. He wishes to point this out through the ways in which we are compelled to make sense of the world in his films.

Another distinctive feature of Wong Kar-wai's cinematic style as seen in *Ashes of Time* is the absence of a unifying viewpoint. This is as much a part of the narrative structure as it is of the visual style, and in the ultimate analysis they are inseparable. There are several reasons for this absence. One is that the voice-overs of the different characters that play such a significant guiding role in the film attests to diversity of viewpoints. In addition, the tension, at times between the word and image, narrative and spectacle, serves to reinforce this. Very often in his films, dominant visual tropes seem to cast a long shadow over the narrative discourse, for example, the revolving bird cage in *Ashes of Time*, the telephone booth in *Days of Being Wild* and the waterfall in *Happy Together*. These dominant tropes can have both a unifying and a disruptive function in terms of the unfolding of the narrative. As a film director, Wong Kar-wai has sought to subvert the practice of maintaining a coherent, unified, and linear narrative with an authoritative viewpoint in favour of a narrative with multiple flexible and disjointed viewpoints.

The performances that the actors and actresses bring to the film are a vital part of Wong's cinematic style. In film after film he employed the same actors and actresses such as Leslie Cheung, Tony Leung Kar-fai, Brigitte Lin Ching-hsia, Tony Leung Chiu-wai, Maggie Cheung and Carina Lau. These actors and actresses, some of the most well-known in Hong Kong and abroad, having acted in Wong Kar-wai's other films have acquired a certain image and aura. What is interesting about Wong Kar-wai as a director is that he desires to tap into this public perception. His approach to actors and acting is very different from that of many of his colleagues in the field of cinema. He is not a great admirer of the Stanislavsky method which encourages actors to get inside the skin of the characters they play by submerging their own personality. He is also not an admirer of the style of acting promoted by Picastor and Brecht, who are associated with the epic theatre. Their objective was to encourage the actors to distance themselves from the roles they were playing to promote a critical outlook in the audiences. Wong Kar-wai, on the contrary, wishes to draw on the public images of his chosen actors and the concomitant cross-identifications so that the public images and the images of the constructed role would generate a new energy. Very often his actors and actresses play against their public persona. This has interesting implications for the evolving meaning of the film. *Ashes of Time*, like all good movies, is not a unitary and closed work, but a diverse and open film that acquires new meanings with the passage of time. One domain in which this takes place is that of the actors' performances. Actors and actresses like Leslie Cheung, Tony Leung Chiu-wai and Maggie Cheung have gone on to act in many of Wong's later films as well as those of other distinguished Hong Kong directors. These later performances cast an interesting light on their earlier performances in *Ashes of Time*. Hence, the way Wong plays the public persona of his actors and actresses against the grain of his projected characters takes on a fascinating dimension of meaning.

The way Wong Kar-wai makes use of stars like Leslie Cheung, Maggie Cheung, Tony Leung Chiu-wai and Brigitte Lin in his films is most interesting, and it is an arena in which he has influenced subsequent film directors. He is fully aware of the implications of stardom in modern commercial film culture and how stardom is located at a complex crossroads of art, popular entertainment, commerce, industry, popular psychology, cultural icons and other factors. Stars can be popular cultural icons, bearers of cultural meaning, performers with distinct public images, commercial attractions and an important element of cinematic meaning. Wong makes use of them as performers who bring their own public persona in to the characters that they are playing in his films and precipitate a tension between their public personas and the nature of the characters that are being played. Wong Kar-wai, more than most other Hong Kong filmmakers, has sought to set in motion this tension, and subsequent directors have found it to be a productive cinematic strategy.

In an interview, Wong categorically stated that he writes scripts with particular actors in mind and that he starts writing only after the main actors and actresses have been identified. This is not uncommon in cinema and even theatre. After all, Shakespeare followed this practice at times. Wong Kar-wai was instrumental in popularizing a certain style of acting. The way he has used stars such as Leslie Cheung, Tony Leung Chiu-wai, Maggie Cheung, Faye Wong, Takeshi Kaneshiro, Andy Lau and Brigitte Lin is indeed interesting. He has forced an acting style out of them that is at once marked by casualness and intensity, attachment and distance, and seriousness and playfulness.

Wong Kar-wai's aim is not merely to tell a story through moving images. He also would like to comment on his very attempt to tell a story. In other words, while seeking to narrate a story through the medium of cinema, he also wishes to look at his own attempt. *Ashes of Time* is not only a narrative about a group of characters encountering a cruel fate. It is also a rumination on a work of cinema that seeks to portray those characters. The way his camera looks at objects, people and events while at the same time looking back on itself illustrates this dual desire of the director. As a film, *Ashes of Time* is not merely the interwoven story of a group of characters that has experienced disappointments in love. He reminds us it is also an artifice, a mechanically constructed film, that aims to deploy all the available resources of cinema. To phrase it differently, Wong's film, while exploring its characters and their destinies, explores itself. This self-reflective approach to film informs his cinematic style.

Wong Kar-wai is a post-MTV film director. He has no compunction in drawing on the ample resources of MTV in making a martial arts film. His camera movements, striking camera angles, abrupt cuts, visual ellipses, sudden dislocations and ingenious use of sound has much in common with the distinguishing attributes of MTV. However, it seems to us that one area in which this is particularly evident is in its editing. In the hands of most film directors, editing has been a mechanism for guiding the audiences in a relatively uncomplicated way through the narrative trajectory of the film. Ambiguities are minimized and narrative comprehension is enhanced through editing to impose a frame of intelligibility. In MTV, on the other hand, editing plays second fiddle to the music and what is of importance is not the content or the sense of what is being seen but the seeing and hearing itself. In other words, the editing associated with MTV has a way of undermining the authority associated with the traditional editing. Consequently, the MTV-inspired filmic text, with its multiple aural and visual signifiers, becomes a medium of complex being seen and hearing. One can see this phenomenon in *Ashes of Time*.

A useful way of approaching the work of Wong Kar-wai is through the notion of *cinecriture* — developed by such theorists as Marie-Claire Ropars-Wuilleumier, which emphasizes the hieroglyphic nature of cinematic signification — cinema that challenges realistic assumptions and mimetic impulses in order to highlight the polysemous nature of cinematic signs.[7] Wong's visual style, then, as manifested in *Ashes of Time* is different from the one that is preferred by most Hong Kong movie-makers. Speaking of Hong Kong cinema, David Bordwell remarked:[8]

> Hong Kong films display some subtle reworkings of classical staging, shooting, and cutting and these contribute to the unique flavor of this popular cinema. For one thing, Hong Kong filmmakers, probably drawing from indigenous Chinese traditions of theatre and martial arts, have developed a rhythmic conception of expressive movement that builds upon the sheerly visceral aspect of cinema's appeal. By presenting a cleanly delineated piece of action, framed at beginning and end by a slight pause, Hong Kong filmmakers have created a distinctive staccato rhythm. This is in turn amplified by color, music, editing, framing, and other film techniques.

Bordwell's description of Hong Kong film style is accurate. What is interesting to note about Wong Kar-wai's style is how far it has deviated from the sanctified norm of Hong Kong filmmaking. What he has attempted to do is to make his visual style an analogue of the fissured and fragmented and dislocated world that he is seeking to depict.

This discussion of Wong's film style should not be construed to mean that it is flawless, and not deficient in any area. This is certainly not the case. There are certain problematic aspects of style in this film. Let us refer to just two examples. We discussed earlier how the voice-overs have become a part of his trademark style, an aspect of his cinematic signature. For example, in *Ashes of Time* four voices are used in the narration without giving adequate information to viewers which voice belongs to which character. This can, at times, prove to be confusing, and foreign audiences have expressly said so. Wong Kar-wai himself admits to this deficiency. He observed, 'That was a serious lesson. The problem did not come to my mind until it was too late. I was doomed with no way out.'

Another deficiency in the film, stylistically speaking, is the excessive compression in the narrative discourse and its visualization. This resulted from his ambition to tell too much in the space available to him. As he himself admitted, one lesson he learned from *Ashes of Time* was that he tried to tell too much with too little space, and it ended up becoming too stylish in storytelling, and that was not his intention.

The above discussion might give the unwarranted impression that Wong Kar-wai is a cerebral filmmaker seeking to establish a thesis and that his intention is only to give free rein to his transgressive desires and iconoclastic ambitions. Nothing could be further from the truth. Despite the fact that *Ashes of Time* is the most forbiddingly and uncompromisingly difficult among his creations to date, he is ultimately interested in pleasing and entertaining audiences. He has stressed in numerous interviews that his aim is to tell a story entertainingly. The fact that this may not have worked in quite the way he intended does not, of course, mean that he has abandoned entertainment. What is of particular interest to most students of cinema is the way in which Wong has instituted a tension between his avant-garde proclivities and the popular roots embedded in cultural memory that are inscribed in his films. He is a thoughtful entertainer who is fully aware of Marcel Duchamp's famous statement that you cannot have a masterpiece without an audience. Reading our discussion of Wong's style, if one is left with the impression that his style has been influenced by filmmakers such as Bresson, Godard, Resnais and Antonioni, the reason for this is because he has. But, at the same time, he has gone beyond them and sought to capture the pulse of the 90s through the visual rhetoric energy of MTV. The way in which he makes use of famous stars, the colours and rhythms of the new media, music and the juxtaposition of images reflects his desire to combine the stylistic signatures of the 60s with the sensuous energies of the 90s. Clearly, this move underlines Wong Kar-wai's desire to create a new category of entertainment. Admittedly, he has been more successful in compelling this interanimation between the avant-garde and the popular in his later work; however, it is not absent from *Ashes of Time*.

7

Martial Arts

Ashes of Time can be loosely termed a *martial arts film*. Hence, in order to understand the film one has to pay close attention to the poetics of this particular genre. Here we are using the term martial arts film to denote a generic category that includes swordfights as well as hand-to-hand combat. There is a certain terminological confusion here that should be clarified. Normally the Cantonese term *wuxia pian* is used to refer to martial arts films with sword fights like King Hu's movies or Ang Lee's popular film *Crouching Tiger, Hidden Dragon*. The term *kung fu* is employed to denote martial arts films containing unarmed combat. The works of Bruce Lee and Jackie Chan belong to this category. This category really became internationally popular in the 1970s. However, outside Hong Kong, and at times inside also, the term kung fu is used to denote films with sword fights as well. Strictly speaking, *Ashes of Time* should be regarded as a *wuxia* film, although many have discussed it as a kung fu film. This confusion itself is a symptom of the transnational nature of Hong Kong cinema and the tendency of Western action films to draw increasingly on the codes and formulas of martial arts films. However, it should be borne in mind that, strictly speaking, kung fu refers to hand-to-hand combat movies and *wuxia* to martial arts films with swordfights. Martial arts films, to much of the outside world, is synonymous with Hong Kong movies in general. When most moviegoers outside of Hong Kong think of Hong Kong cinema, what immediately comes to mind is the heroics of martial arts films. As with any film genre, there are different sub-categories within the general rubric. In the case of martial arts movies, there are films devoted to sword fighting and horsemanship, hand-to-hand combat, comedies, techno-fantasy versions and so on. Martial arts movies have evolved during the past eighty years, responding to new challenges and absorbing new elements and also reshaping those elements. They also have become interesting sites that reflect the commerce, the imperatives of the national imaginary, and the dynamics of the transnational space of cinema.

Before we attempt to explore the nature and significance of martial arts movies, it is useful to pay some attention to the idea of a film genre. The martial arts film is a distinct film genre in the sense that westerns, musicals, horror films, film noir and science fiction films are different Western film genres. Cinema can best be understood as a social practice in which the art, entertainment, industrial, technological and ideological aspects are combined to form a complex unity. In other words, we need to pay close attention to the idea of cinema as a social institution. According to the eminent film theorist Christian Metz, the cinematic institution consists of not only the cinema industry but also the mental machinery; mental machinery is understood as the way in which moviegoers historically have internalized the conventions of cinema and as moviegoers' orientation towards the consumption of films. Genres can be regarded as important elements of this machinery. According to Stephen Neale, genres are 'systematized forms of the articulation of meaning and position. They are a fundamental part of the cinema's mental machinery. Approached in this way, genres are not to be seen as forms of textual codifications, but as systems of orientations, expectations, and conventions that circulate between industry, text and subject.'[1] This encapsulation of the essential features of a filmic genre enables us to understand better the ontology of martial arts movies.

The martial arts are closely linked to the deepest wellsprings of Chinese culture. Originally, the term kung fu designated not a form of martial art but the undertaking and completion of daunting tasks. It indicated a certain attitude of mind and a disciplining of the body. According to legend, Bodhidharma who was involved in the propagation of Buddhism in China came to the famous Shaolin monastery. It is here — a monastery well-known for the translation of Buddhist scriptures — that kung fu took root. As with all legends, this one too points towards an important historical fact — in this case, the deep religious and cultural roots of this art form.

As far as cinema is concerned, martial arts movies began to be produced in mainland China in the 1920s. They were designated by the compound phrase *wuxia shenguai pian* which literally meant 'martial arts–magic spirit films'. At first they generated a great measure of enthusiasm among audiences, bringing a new sense of cinematic excitement. For a short while, this new form of film entertainment dominated cinema. At this early stage of martial arts filmmaking, martial arts movies were heavily influenced by the aesthetics and codes of representation and rhetorical strategies of stage plays. However, this new found enthusiasm did not last long, and the enthusiasm for these films began to wane very quickly. There was also a strong reaction from certain quarters of society which saw them as promoting a retrogressive glorification of feudal values at the expense of social progress.

It was only in the 50s, with the *Huang Feihung* film series that kung fu movies sprang back into life. And this time it was in Hong Kong. Between 1949 and 1959, nearly 70 episodes of the *Huang Feihung* series were produced. There had been some years when there had been a great upsurge in production as, for example, in 1956 when as many as twenty-five *Huang Feihung* films were made. This film series succeeded in giving a strong boost to the Hong Kong film industry, infusing it with a new vigour and the films with a broad-based appeal. *Huang Feihung* began to lose some of its attracting power in the 1970s, although they continued to be made until the 1980s. Nearly one hundred episodes of the *Huang Feihung* series were made, marking them as constituting a significant stage in the growth of Hong Kong's visual entertainment industry.

These films are important not only on account of their promoting the kung fu tradition in Hong Kong and generating an interest in kung fu abroad, but also creating a distinct image of this form and displaying its cinematic possibilities. In particular, a certain kind of easily recognizable hero, who was strongly motivated and capable of enlisting the admiration of the majority of moviegoers emerged. He was idolized as he sought to live by and disseminate community-sanctioned values. He was a respecter of tradition, an upholder of cultural norms, altruistic, generous, quick to react to injustices and to rectify them; he came to the aid of the powerless and downtrodden, took extra care not to yield to sexual desire, and led a disciplined life. As we shall presently see, the protagonist of *Ashes of Time* represents a very different type of person in comparison to the protagonists in run-of-the-mill kung fu and *wuxia* movies.

Martial arts movies were invested with a new vibrancy in the late 1960s and 1970s with the work of King Hu, and Zhang Che who sought to revitalize the martial arts genre. As King Hu is the better known of the two internationally, we will to focus on his work. King Hu attempted to draw on the representational strategies, visuals and sounds of Peking Opera as well traditional Chinese paintings to create a martial arts film tradition that emphasized the poetry of physical motion. A highly acclaimed film like *A Touch of Zen* illustrates this point. The idea of heroism and nobility of spirit is central to the larger ambitions of martial arts movies and the Shaw Brothers film company played a crucial role in winning recognition popularity for this genre. When King Hu's films such as *Come Drink With Me* began to do well at the box-office, it was evident that this form had struck a deep chord with the average moviegoer. Towards the latter part of this chapter, we hope to focus more on King Hu's films because Wong Kar-wai, in making his martial arts film, was inspired by and reacting against King Hu's films. In the 1970s, Bruce Lee gave an added impetus to kung fu films by investing them with certain elements that had a transnational appeal. He succeeded in making kung fu movies relevant to contemporary times by infusing them with a sense of modernity even as he focused on the importance of patriotism and the discursive constructions of Chinese greatness. He focused on the male body in novel ways by making clever use of the apparatus of cinema. And what is interesting to note here is that he focused on the male body as away of drawing attention to the idea of nationhood and its significance in the national imaginary. Films such as *Fist of Fury* and *The Way of the Dragon* served to promote a discourse of nationhood on the basis of the power of the male body. It is also interesting to observe that a new hybrid quality was added to kung fu movies with the work of Bruce Lee. As critics like Lo Kwai-cheung have pointed out, although he focused on issues of Chineseness and nationhood and patriotism, he himself was an American citizen, born in California and had an Eurasian mother.[2] And biographical factors have a way of intervening in the cultural products of entertainment in interesting ways.

The next stage in the development of Hong Kong martial arts movies is marked by the emergence of Jackie Chan. He succeeded Bruce Lee, who died in 1973, as the leading figure associated with martial arts films. He introduced a note of comedy that was not widely present in earlier kung fu films. The image of the hero, too, underwent a change, signifying an important departure from the past. While focusing on the elements of physicality and performance of stunts, he introduced an element of the slapstick which had a transformative effect on the genre. And instead of portraying patriots and men of indefatigable valour, he brought to the screen characters that were ordinary and even vulnerable. In films like *Drunken Master* and *Snake in the Eagle Shadows*, one sees the trademark features of Jackie Chan's art. With the work of Bruce Lee and Jackie Chan, martial arts films began to exercise a greater influence on the imagination of Western audiences. In the 1990s there was a revival of the swordplay films, notably with the launching of the *Swordsman* film series. Today, martial arts films have become a worldwide phenomenon, generating interest among moviegoers in America, Europe, Asia and Latin America and inflecting the global vocabulary of action films the world over. The recent spectacular success of Ang Lee's swordfight film *Crouching Tiger, Hidden Dragon* generated an unprecedented interest in martial arts films in the West, and Zhang Yimou's latest film, *Hero*, promises to intensify that interest. Interestingly, the dynamics of the martial arts movies are now being absorbed by Hollywood films such as *The Matrix*, *Tomb Raider* and *Charlie's Angels*. This reflects the power of globalization as well as the technologization and transnationalization of the martial arts film.

There are several significant turning points in the evolution of *wuxia* martial arts films in Hong Kong in the 1990s. The *Swordsman* series produced by Tsui Hark is one such point. The making of *Once Upon a Time in China* series by Tsui Hark is another. Tsui Hark's first *Once Upon a Time in China* is a beautifully made film that uses the resources of the martial arts genre and new technological developments in cinematography to focus on the issues of nationhood, imperialism, colonialism, modernity and the complexities of nation-building. The third significant point is the making of Wong Kar-wai's *Ashes of Time* — the subject of this volume.

It is against this backdrop of the growth of the martial arts movie tradition in Hong Kong that we have to examine *Ashes of Time*. It is indeed a *wuxia* movie with a difference. Wong Kar-wai, in a very skillful way, makes use of the representational codes, the markers and the authority of the genre only to undercut it and subvert it from within.

Let us first consider the character of Ouyang Feng. In a typical martial arts film, as we observed earlier, the protagonist embodies the socially valorized norms and modes of behaviour. He embodies heroism and is a wholly admirable figure representing the best of his community. He is motivated by lofty goals, whether they be to stand up for the nation or to undo social injustices. One can see these traits in the *Huang Feihung* movies as well as in the work of King Hu. In *Ashes of Time*, on the other hand, Ouyang Feng waits in a desert as lonely as it is vast and barren, making his living as an agent for killers. He is a death-broker — something that would be totally repugnant to the majority of martial arts heroes. He has no noble aims or objectives other than making money. He is guided solely by crass self-interest. His cynical and mercenary interests are clearly reflected in his statement, when speaking to a potential client, 'Buddy, you must be around forty. In forty years, you must have come to hate someone, someone who wronged you, someone you wanted to kill ... Murder can be very simple ... I've this friend who's skilled in martial arts ... Pay a fee and he'll kill for you.'

Ouyang, unlike the typical *wuxia* hero, has no heroic ambitions. Indeed, to him, heroic acts are meaningless. His primary aim is to make a living as a cynical mercenary. When people who are poor and helpless come to him for assistance, as in the case of the peasant girl with a basket of eggs who wants the killers of her brother to be brought to justice, he turns the other way. If she had enough money, he certainly would have undertaken the job. Chivalry, which is intrinsic to the world of traditional martial arts movie heroes has no resonance in the small world that Ouyang inhabits. He is self-centered, miserly, opportunistic and manipulative just like his friend, the other swordsman, Huang Yaoshi.

Hong Qi is the only character in *Ashes of Time* who aspires to be a famous swordsman in the tradition of *wuxia* heroes. He also displays a sense of humanity and generosity, conspicuously lacking in the other three male heroes in *Ashes of Time*. He is so moved by the request of the peasant girl with the basket of eggs that he decides to take on the cruel warriors for the price of a mere egg — something that earns him the opprobrium of Ouyang. In the fight he loses one of his fingers but succeeds in vanquishing his adversaries. Even Hong Qi, however, does not measure up to the exalted standards of martial arts heroes. He is poor, barefooted, travels on a camel and is accompanied by his wife in his martial adventures — hardly the ideal master swordsmen heroes of Chinese swordplay movies. Although Hong Qi does not possess some of the despicable features of the other three heroes in the film, even he falls far short of the mark in heroism and nobility associated with protagonists of martial arts movies.

There are other significant differences between *Ashes of Time* and other martial arts films. In most martial arts films, time is filled with heroic action; action, which is daring and presented in a stylized form, is the narrative anchor in these films. And action is time, time is action. The protagonists define themselves through action and spend their time pursuing their destinies through action. In the case of *Ashes of Time*, the opposite is true Ouyang and the other characters spend their time waiting for action; much of the film's length is made up of waiting. In most martial arts films there is a vital interanimation between space and time — physical space is a site for displaying action. On the other hand, there is a different connection between space and time in *Ashes of Time*. Both point to the dead weight of time and inactive, brooding, reflective and manipulative characters removed from action. When *Ashes of Time* was first shown in Hong Kong in 1994, many of the viewers felt disappointed and let down because the film did not conform to the prevalent image of martial arts movies. The un-heroic heroes and the lack of pervasive action were primarily responsible for the audience's disenchantment. In contrast to the typical martial arts movies, there is a striking relationship between time and waiting in *Ashes of Time* which reminds one of Blanchot's statement that 'waiting is when time is always in excess and when time is nevertheless short on time. The overabundant lack of time is the duration of waiting.'[3]

The idea of community is another point of difference between *Ashes of Time* and other martial arts films. The ostentatious heroism of martial arts film protagonists emerges from, and is vitally connected to, the idea of a community — the idea of a group of people living in a common space sharing common traditions, values and lifestyles. These heroes incarnate the most cherished values that bind the community together, and their struggles are, in the final analysis, in the service of that community. The heroes of *Ashes of Time* represent the antithesis of this desideratum. They are unmoored from their community, each pursuing his own private goals and interests. Far from being noble heroes with exalted ambitions, they are, to use a word from the film, 'wounded souls' who are weighed down by private failures and dejections. The vast desert with its empty radiance, the expansive ocean with its rolling waves and the distant and timeless mountains signify the heroes' lack of connection with a flourishing community. The idea of the absence of a community has another facet of meaning in relation to this film. As Walter Benjamin pointed out in his essay on the storyteller, the ability share a common fund of experience and to narrate it in a commonly intelligible idiom brings about a community. There was a martial arts film community based on this line of reasoning that was familiar with the codes, signs, conventions, and values inherent in the genre. However, Wong Kar-wai, in *Ashes of Time,* destabilized this community by turning his back on the common narrative and experiential framework.

As we stated earlier *Ashes of Time* contains a syntactic diversity that has the effect of partially distancing the spectator from the textualized experience. This is in contrast to traditional martial arts films that are simpler in their narrative trajectory and very often operate on a single plane of meaning. The simplicity of the narrative structure constitutes part of the appeal of martial arts movies. In *Ashes of Time* the cinematic experience operates at a number of levels of significance, urging the viewer to shift his viewpoints and enhancing the symbolic density of the narrative. In the average martial arts film we reconstruct characters and situations on the basis of the clear evidence presented by the director in a readily understandable form. Here, Wong Kar-wai displays some affinity to King Hu's movies, which will be discussed later. In most martial arts films, the perception of characters and situations grows out of a faith in the unquestioned authority of the narrative. In *Ashes of Time,* with its complex narrative structure, disruptions of diegetic unity, self-doubts and self-interrogations, that faith in the authority of the narrative is undermined. This, along with the author's relentless attempts to explore the semiotic and significative possibilities of cinema while narrating a story, results in the partial distancing of the spectator that we referred to earlier. To give an example from the film, contrary to typical martial arts movies in which the ending is carefully guarded till the end, in *Ashes of Time*, the characters (and the spectators) are made aware at the beginning of what their destinies will be. The opening words of Ouyang are, 'In the years to come I will be given the nickname Malicious West,' thus giving away the conclusion.

In general, martial arts films operate at the level of a morality play which stages a conflict between good and evil, and the protagonist almost always represents the good while his adversaries incarnate the power of evil. There is no doubt as to who enlists the admiration of the spectators. In Wong Kar-wai's film, on the contrary, there are no good protagonists. All of them are highly vulnerable creatures who are suffering from past errors of judgment and behaviour. Hence one does not see the kind of straightforward clash of good and evil that characterizes many of the martial arts movies. Wong is too talented a film director to submit to such an elementary binarism. His radical disjunctions between word and image, narrative and spectacle, and action and reaction complicate the situation further. In both *wuxia* and kung fu movies in general, the moral order that is temporarily unsettled is restored through the valiant struggles of the protagonists. However, in *Ashes of Time,* the moral order, which is nebulous to start with, is further plunged into incomprehensible uncertainties.

The sword is the symbol of the nobility and valour dramatized in martial arts films. It is, of course, a symbol of phallic power as well. The culture inhabited by martial arts film protagonists has been written by and for men. In *Ashes of Time*, Ouyang has decided to give up the sword signifying the castration of the phallus. This is a symbolism that goes against the tenor of *wuxia* films. Moreover, the sword, which was a symbol of grandeur and nobility, has in *Ashes of Time* become a signifier of crass self-interest. As Stephen Ching-kiu Chan has pointed out, in this film the use of the sword is motivated not by the lofty ideals of passion or rectification of injustice but to kill people for money.[4] Swordplay, which was the emotional and dramatic center of martial arts movies, has been transformed in this film into a mercenary enterprise, resulting in the shattering of a long established cultural world.

The topos of nostalgia figures prominently in most, if not all, traditional martial arts movies. Etymologically, nostalgia indexes the longing for a lost home. In the case of martial arts movies it is a longing for a mythical past in which there was no confusion about moral values and the distinction between good and evil was simple and clear. However, in the case of *Ashes of Time*, a martial arts movie with a difference, moral values are in a state of confusion and the world is never lucid and transparent as in traditional martial arts films. The nostalgia in this case is for an ideal and non-historical space in which perfect communication is possible; in other words, an impossible longing.

The martial arts films, like any other film genre, is a product of distinct social and cultural contexts. The films of the fifties projected a longing for a mythical past that reflected the country's unease with the current colonial rule. King Hu's movies of the 60s glorified the richness of classical Chinese culture. Movies in the 70s reflected the growing hybridization of Hong Kong and the search for roots. Jackie Chan in the 1980s introduced a new note of comedy that had much to do with the relaxation of tensions in China, and the opening up of the Mainland to the West. Against this background, what is interesting to note about Wong Kar-wai's martial arts film is that it recognizes the impossibility of looking back to any glorious past and confronts modern modes of feeling and sensibility with all their intransigent complexities. In some ways it is an allegory of the spread of capitalism with its demonstration of the power of money. One can argue that this structure of feeling relates to the increasing importance of Hong Kong as a global financial center.

Despite all the variations, Hong Kong martial arts films constitute a recognizable genre. The modes of style and presentation, the semiotics of action, the visual rhetoric and the entertainment are intimately bound up with physical movement. These films highlight the power, beauty and agility of the human body, while the fight sequences are most often choreographed in a way that emphasizes the poetry of movement. Increasingly, special effects are being deployed to ensure the maximum effect in underlining these movements. These are fast-paced films in which one action sequence follows another in breathless succession. We find the use of special effects in *Ashes of Time* as well. However, in this case, the objective is not to obtain maximum profile for the actors or to enhance the intensity of the action, but rather to call attention to the limitations of specularity itself and the formal and stylistic qualities that one normally associates with martial arts movies. Therefore, the question naturally arises, what motivated Wong Kar-wai to make use of this genre? What advantages and benefits does he gain by such a choice? Here we wish to focus on what we think are two important aspects. First, an identifying mark of any film genre is that it generates certain expectations in the minds of audiences. Genres share certain basic attributes and establish a bond with the spectators in terms of expectations and cultural expressivities. For example, martial arts movies generally focus on action, noble and admirable heroes, culturally sanctioned values and so on. In the case of *Ashes of Time* all such expectations are undermined. The intention of the director is to give greater definition to the experience he is communicating and the characters he is portraying, by contrasting them with other movies of the genre and the expectations that animate the audiences. It is almost as if the majority of martial arts movies constitute the 'other' against which his film gains its individuality. It is a rewriting of the genre with contemporary imperatives in mind.

The second aspect has to do with the question of ideology. One of the functions of ideology, whether it be in society in general, or in cultural texts in particular, is to present as natural and inevitable what is constructed and contrived. In the case of martial arts movies, the neat unities and the coherent visages of these films conceal a repressive ideology that glorifies social order over individual desire. The heroes with all their admirable social and personal attributes come to emblematize the essence of that social order. The hapless victims, the dispossessed seeking justice, the victimized and the harassed become mirrors in which the heroes are reflected and consequently glorified. It is a world that beckons heroes and glory is the watchword. And there is the constant approbation of the community to the good deeds of the heroes. In addition, the world of martial arts movies is a world in which patriarchy rules. In *Ashes of Time*, on the other hand, there is an attempt to deconstruct the patriarchal hegemony, although not successfully, and to unmask the ideologies that govern peoples' lives. Moreover, traditional martial arts movies are predictable and therefore induce a sense of social containment. Despite the continual flash and fire, in the final analysis the martial arts movie constitutes a cinema of security. Wong's *Ashes of Time*, on the other hand, defeats that predictability and thereby shatters the sense of security to open up a contested space for agonized self-reflection. Therefore, the departure from the ambitions and discursive specifications of martial arts movies enables Wong Kar-wai to move towards uncovering the regimes of ideology that govern society as well as cultural texts.

Third, the idea of chronotope as enunciated by Mikhail Bakhtin is important in understanding the disparities between *Ashes of Time* and other martial arts movies.[5] Chronotopes focus on the complex relationship between time and space in any given cultural geography. It is a useful way of understanding the determinants of social living. Different film genres entertain different chronotopes. Most martial arts movies operate on the basis of linear time frames and unproblematized spaces. They stage their experiences on a unilevelled narrative trajectory. *Ashes of Time*, on the other hand, deals with recursive and circular time and constantly seeks to problematize the space its characters inhabit by playing off the themes of absence and presence, forgetting and remembering. Moreover, the unspecified time in which the action takes place and the contemporary sensibility that informs the story serve to problematize the simple and univocal chronotopes depicted in martial arts films.

In terms of visual style, there are clear differences between *Ashes of Time* and the majority of martial arts films. In the latter, the issue of forceful, unimpeded and clear visibility is of the essence.

The focus of the camera is on the human body and the actions performed by it. Very often the action takes place in a clearly demarcated and limited space. To follow the story is to follow the bodies in action. The long shot and the medium long shot, with their emphasis on action, are constantly employed by the directors. The objective of camerawork is to intensify the emotions generated through action by maximizing the visibility. In the case of *Ashes of Time* the opposite is the case; as Abbas has pointed out, it is the invisibility that dominates the fight sequences rather than the much sought-after visibility.[6] Very often the action has been speeded up to a blur.

One of the central questions any discerning viewer is likely to ask of *Ashes of Time* is why the director chose to press into service the martial arts form. What are the tangible pay-offs? One has to confront this question if one is to comprehend the full force of meaning generated by the complex entanglements between sign and desire. It is our conviction that Wong Kar-wai wanted to deconstruct the martial arts genre; to deconstruct is not to destroy but to displace the mode of enunciation and address a different space, a space of alterity. In this effort, he demonstrates both the fragility and resilience of the form. It also reflects a desire to dialecticize the genre.

In order to examine the implications of Wong Kar-wai's movie, we need to focus firstly on the idea of cinematic genre and its position within specific regimes of signification. Although the word 'genre' refers to a way of organizing films according to type, it is vitally connected with codified viewer expectations, circulation of signs, issues of production, marketing and consumption, as well as questions of narrative, characterization, iconography, visual rhetoric, stardom, codes and conventions, productions of meaning, etc. But we also need to remember that genres develop dialogically within specific cultural horizons as ways of inflecting social experience and recasting them in the accepted vocabulary of imagination. This point takes on a particular resonance in the work of Wong as exemplified in *Ashes of Time*.

The highly stylized gestures, narrative and visual codes, camera placements and movements, lighting, editing, iconography, *mise en scene*, strategies of authentication, structures of alignment and intertextual plenitude associated with the traditional martial arts movies have been displaced. This is a way of undermining the authority of the form and clearing a new space of enunciation and address. This, of course, involves the navigation of a tortuous path between identification and cognition, belief and disbelief, and attachment and distance. The transgressive impulses of the film, as they collide with the set boundaries of the martial arts genre, and resulting in the film's displacement of itself, are a fascinating aspect of the film. Although Wong does not go far enough in this direction, *Ashes of Time* shows us the desirability and the feasibility of uncovering ideological presuppositions at work in consensual forms like martial arts films. He exposes how *Ashes* seeks to mask the contingency of its constructive energies with a naturalized orthodoxy. Ultimately, what is significant about Wong's effort is his success in rewriting the martial arts genre so as to permit the articulation of a distinctively modern form of imagination. Indeed, the intention of the film is to make the martial arts film form an enabling condition for giving definition to idioms of modern sensibility, and in turn use of these idioms as an enabling condition for giving definition to the martial arts film form, resulting in the release of deconstructive energies. In *Ashes of Time*, Wong Kar-wai has sought to re-explore and redraw the semiotic map in which the martial arts form has been securely located.

So far we have discussed *Ashes of Time* against the backdrop of martial arts films in general. However, it is not a simple opposition between *Ashes of Time* and the martial arts film genre. Filmmakers such as King Hu complicate this neatly laid out picture. Indeed, the relationship between Wong and Hu is a complex one.

On the one hand, Wong is impressed by Hu's powerful visual imagination and the apparent ease with which Hu handled the form. On the other hand, Wong Kar-wai wishes to deconstruct and dismantle the martial arts form of filmmakers such as King Hu from within. Both Hu and Wong's works reflect their deep interest in the widening of the discursive boundaries of the martial arts form using the available resources of cinema. While Hu wished to do so by exploiting to the full the resources of the form, Wong is interested in subverting it from within.

There are many similarities between King Hu and Wong Kar-wai. King Hu was interested in lonely travelers, exiles and nomads and this is what we find in *Ashes of Time* as well. The stories of *Come Drink With Me* and *The Wheel of Life* take place in isolated huts, *A Touch of Zen* takes place in a thick forest while the story of *Raining in the Mountains* is set in a Buddhist monastery. King Hu, though not a Buddhist himself, was deeply influenced by Chan Buddhism. His film *All the King's Men* begins with a Buddhist reciting from the scriptures. Similarly, we find a Chan Buddhist speaking at the beginning of Wong's film. King Hu was greatly interested in the fluidity of action and the poetry of movement, and at times rhythmic movements took precedence over the powerful and uncomplicated representation of the body. We find this same desire in Wong Kar-wai's film as well. King Hu, despite his great attachment to, and respect for classical Chinese culture was not afraid to use Western music in his martial arts films when it suited his designs, as in *Raining in the Mountain* and *The Valiant Ones*. In some of his films, King Hu employed music not only to strengthen the visuals but also to challenge them and to extend them. This desire can be observed in Wong's films as well. King Hu, in keeping with his Chan Buddhist inclinations, valued experiential immediacy over cognition and ratiocination. We find this in Wong's films as well. Hu often created mind-independent worlds and adopted changing representational perspectives to capture the elusive truths about that world. This is a vision that finds an echo in Wong as well. One sees, then, a number of similarities between King Hu and Wong Kar-wai. The question therefore, is why would Wong Kar-wai want to deconstruct a form, at least as represented in the work of King Hu, that he so greatly admires. The answer to that question lies in the fact that we deconstruct best what we admire most.

There are, of course, clear differences between the two directors as well. Wong has a preference for an existentialism, at times bordering on nihilism, that one does not find in Hu. Despite his attraction to multifaceted narratives, King Hu always maintained a clear plot line in his martial arts films, which is certainly not the case in *Ashes of Time*. Moreover there is a predilection for metaphysics that one does not find in Wong. Despite the very dexterous use of spatiality and innovative inter-splicing in King Hu's films, they do not focus on the discontinuities and dislocations in the way that Wong's films do. For King Hu, fragmentation has no positive connotations or valences. There is a sense of the sublime in many of King Hu's movies as well as in *Ashes of Time*, However, there is a difference — in King Hu's case it is a positive sublimity while in the case of Wong Kar-wai it is attained through negativity. King Hu sought to draw audiences emotionally into the predicaments of his characters while it is the aim of Wong to put a distance between the characters and the viewers. Wong has also sought to draw on westerns as a way of enriching the martial arts form in a way that Hu did not. By his own admission, *Ashes of Time* was influenced by John Ford's *The Searchers*. The way Wong Kar-wai deploys the martial arts form, the way he extends its range by destabilizing it, is not a simple tale of the rejection of a genre, but the complicated story of the assimilation of a genre, the transgression of a genre and deep engagement with a genre. Wong's intention has been to uncover the ideological syntax of the martial arts film form — something that never was a priority for King Hu.

Unlike Hu, Wong seeks to display and displace the visage of the martial arts film in his attempt at a transgressive rewriting of the genre.

Our discussion of Wong Kar-wai and martial arts movies should not lead to the erroneous conclusion that he is the only director who has sought to re-invent the martial arts film genre for modern times. In the 1990s there was revival of interest in the martial arts genre thanks to the innovative work of such directors as Tsui Hark, Ching Siu-tung and Raymond Lee. *Once Upon a Time in China*, made in 1991, and *Once Upon a Time in China II*, made in 1992, — both directed by Tsui Hark — are most interesting in this regard. They are visually captivating films that utilize the full resources of cinema to create martial arts films that appeal to a contemporary sensibility. In terms of themes, they open up issues regarding imperialism, patriotism, nationhood, technology and others in compelling ways. Similarly, the *Swordsman* series of films invite closer study. *Swordsman* was made in 1990, *Swordsman II* in 1991 and *Swordsman III* was made in 1993. All three *Swordsman* films were produced by Tsui Hark. The first *Swordsman*, based on a novel by Jin Yong, deals with an internecine struggle among diverse martial arts clans to secure a scroll that possesses magical powers. Imaginatively choreographed fight sequences using the latest technologies invest the film, and the other two films in the series, with an intense visual power. *Swordsman II*, which is a loose continuation of the previous film, deals with power struggles and intrigue using the machinery of cinema to great effect. For example, some of the sequences that contain wire-enhanced choreographies of fighting are unsurpassed in their compelling visuals. *Swordsman III* which is also called *East is Red* tells a story, originating from the earlier work, about plans to take possession of the world with Spanish warships and Japanese submarines.

All these films made in the 1990s invigorated the swordplay genre and succeeded in displaying their contemporary appeal. Some of them pointed in the direction of international politics, and, in this sense, they have a greater topical interest than *Ashes of Time*. Moreover, many of these films sought to interrogate and transform certain aspects of the swordplay films that were in circulation in the 1960s. For example, the idea of the sustaining cultural space and a distinct world of imagination or *jianghu* is central to this genre. *Jianghu* literally refers to three rivers and five lakes in mainland China. Its real significance lies in the fact that it indicates the self-contained and historically sanctioned world of martial arts. The concept of heroism, vital to the swordplay genre, is inseparably linked to this concept and one feeds off the other. Filmmakers such as Tsui Hark and Wong Kar-wai, each in their own ways, sought to reinterpret the idea of *jianghu* and its associated heroism in the light of modern sensibilities. However, despite the fact that Tsui Hark, Ching Siu-tung and Raymond Lee re-invigorated the martial arts film form before Wong Kar-wai, there are clear differences between them and Wong. Wong's film, though not totally free of the workings of fantasy, is much less under the sway of fantasy than the other martial arts films made in the 1990s. Despite certain doubts and hesitancies, a residual sense of heroism is still vital to them in a way that it is not in the case with *Ashes of Time*. Moreover, they are all action-oriented films, whereas *Ashes of Time* is much more a reflective and meditative film. A deep moral imagination courses through the earlier *wuxia* films made in the 1990s. It is not an animating force in *Ashes of Time*. Many of the swordplay films of the last decade showed how heroism is exemplified, while Wong indicated how banality is lived. Furthermore, despite the ramifications of the story, the *Once Upon a Time in China* films and the *Swordsman* series point to coherence in narrative and style. In contrast, in our discussions of the narrative structure and style of *Ashes of Time*, we sought to point out how coherence is for Wong a dubious virtue and an ambiguous goal. The self-critical gaze on the world and the cultural space of the martial arts films characterizes Wong's approach; he prefers this approach largely because he wants to prevent his works from becoming static epistemological objects.

Another useful way of situating Wong Kar-wai in the evolving tradition of martial arts filmmaking is to consider the concept of *jianghu* which is at the heart of this genre. In martial arts films the term *jianghu* indicates the world 'out there' as opposed to home. It refers to an imaginary world of signification that operates under the sign of swordplay films. The word 'topos', with its dual meanings of place and topic, it seems to us, enables us to capture the essence of this concept well. Commentators like Lin Nien-tung have identified three phases through which this concept has evolved in Hong Kong cinema. In the first phase, beginning in the 1950s, this cultural thought-world was traversed by magical and supernatural forces, investing the characters with superhuman abilities. The late 60s marks the second phase with the advent of filmmakers such as King Hu and Zhang Che who invested the *jianghu* with the desires and ambitions of ordinary people living in a political world. The third stage, which began in the 70s, reached a high point in the late 80s and 90s when films began to question and challenge the traditionally grounded *jianghu* and its concomitant chivalry. One of the earliest and most significant films representative of this latest stage is Tsui Hark's *Butterfly Murders*, made in 1979, which marked his directorial debut. The film combines the martial arts genre with the power of horror and mystery films. The focus of the film, interestingly, is not on a lonely, nomadic swordsman, as is typically the case in swordplay films, but a peripatetic writer. *Swordsman II*, produced by Tsui Hark and directed by Ching Siu-tung, which we discussed earlier, also represents some of the noteworthy developments in the third phase. It is against this backdrop that we have to consider how Wong Kar-wai's *Ashes of Time* challenges the *jianghu* in a fundamental way by destabilizing the humanist measure of things. He has sought to effect a cultural and epistemic redefinition of *jianghu* by focusing on immanence, indeterminacy and nihilism to jolt us to a new awareness of ourselves and the martial arts form. His new approach to *jianghu* reveals a new world that in turn reveals the *jianghu*.

Finally, we wish to call attention to the question of feminism and the martial arts form. Despite the best efforts of Tsui Hark and Wong Kar-wai, the patriarchal imperatives of the genre remain intact in this genre. Tsui Hark focused on transgressions and ambiguities of gender, while Wong through his characters like Murong Yin, Ouyang Feng's girlfriend and the peasant girl gestured towards the acquisition of female agency. In more recent times, films have given important fighting roles to leading female stars such as Michelle Yeoh in *Crouching Tiger, Hidden Dragon*. Yet the fact remains that in these films, the narrative discourse comes to life and achieves definition under the sign of a patriarchal dispensation.

This chapter is the longest in the book, and with reason. At the outset, we said that our aim was to situate *Ashes of Time* in its historical, cultural, and conceptual context as a way of understanding the film. Reading the film within the evolving framework of martial arts films in Hong Kong, we believe, enables us to accomplish that task.

8

Time

A useful pathway to understanding *Ashes of Time* is the concept of time with all its complex and convoluted philosophical ramifications. The English title of the film clearly emphasizes the significance of time, while the Chinese title, roughly translated as *Malevolent East, Malicious West*, focuses on the concept of space. Much of the film is devoted to explorations of memory and desire entangled with time. There are intense moments of action interspersed with long periods of inactivity and waiting. Indeed, one of the visual strengths of the film, and the high points of Christopher Doyle's camerawork, is the memorable depiction of these moments of stasis. The weight of dead time is clearly and agonizingly felt by many of the characters in *Ashes of Time*. The well-known film critic Tony Rayns calls Wong Kar-wai a 'poet of time'. According to him, no other filmmaker since Alain Resnais has been so attuned to the impact of time on memory, sensation and emotion. As he remarked, 'Few other directors have ever imbibed their movies with such a metaphysical sense of time at work: dilating, stretching, lurching, dragging, speeding by.'[1]

Jacques Derrida, the great deconstructive philosopher, has

some insightful observations on ashes and cinder, which hold a relevance to the present discussion of Wong Kar-wai's film. He once remarked, 'I would prefer ashes as the better paradigm for what I call the trace — something that erases itself totally, radically, while presenting itself.'[2] Anyone familiar with Derrida's expositions on deconstructive analyses would realize the central role that the idea of 'trace' plays in them. It is Derrida's belief that to hear, to speak and to write is to experience the heat and the retreat of the fire as the cinder falls, once more, to ash. According to him, cinder is 'that which preserves in order no longer to preserve'.[3] This statement encapsulates in a particularly vivid manner the dilemma confronting many of the characters in *Ashes of Time*. All the main characters, it becomes evident as the story unfolds, seek to preserve time in order not to preserve it. Hence, the English title of the film is extremely suggestive of the complexities expressed in the film.

The question of time is deeply inscribed both in the context and style of *Ashes of Time*. Indeed, Wong is a filmmaker deeply concerned with time. The very titles of his films, *As Tears Go By*, *Days of Being Wild*, *Ashes of Time*, *Chungking Express*, *Happy Together* and *In the Mood for Love*, call attention to the temporal and the transitory. The protagonist of *Ashes of Time*, Ouyang Feng, constantly refers to almanacs and calendars, and in his voice-overs there are numerous references to seasons and time. The voice-overs are like diaries which record the passing of time. Hence, time is a significant point of reference to the characters as well as a heavy burden to be carried. Simultaneously, there are obvious contradictions in the understanding and calibration of time. For example, in the voice-over narration we hear, 'day six (insects awaken)', followed by, 'day four (first day in spring)'. Similarly, day 15 is alluded to twice: once as 'sunny and windy' and later as 'rainy'. Such discrepancies in the characterization and delineation of time are reconfigured in the visual imagery. At times, some of the characters in the film are unable to pin down time, resulting in vague and uncertain articulations such as 'a few years later', 'three years later' and 'ever since that night'.

The narrative structure, just like the modes of enunciation, highlight the complex and ambiguous relationship with time experienced by the characters. *Ashes of Time* is a film many viewers feel the need to discuss because it is difficult to understand. This difficulty arises partly from the polymorphous nature of time as registered in the consciousness of such characters as Ouyang Feng, Huang Yaoshi and the Sunset Warrior. There are flashbacks within flashbacks, shifts of viewpoint, startling juxtapositions of events and fragmented scenes that constitute a vital aspect of Wong Kar-wai's narrative discourse and process of expression. This narrative structure is discernible not only in *Ashes of Time* but also in his other movies such as *Days of Being Wild*, *As Tears Go By*, *Fallen Angels*, *Chungking Express* and *Happy Together*. The emphasis on fragmented narrative structure and visual reconfiguration is closely tied to Wong Kar-wai's vision of time. We will have more to say on the importance of fragmentation to his film aesthetics in a later chapter.

The main dramatis personae in *Ashes of Time* are victims of time. They are unable to master time or even to understand its tormenting power. Ouyang Feng, Huang Yaoshi, Murong Yin/Yang, the Sunset Warrior and the former girlfriend of Ouyang are trapped in memory. Memory, both through its process of selective remembering and selective forgetting, destroys and preserves time. Hence, it can legitimately be said that time is a strong determinant of their subjectivities. There are echoes and re-echoes of earlier statements and emotions, duplications of earlier events, revisits to identical locations and replays of the same actions or inactions which all testify to the power of time. Every spring, Huang visits Ouyang at his inn in the desert. The peasant girl with the basket of eggs implores all passing swordsman to avenge the death of her brother by taking on the cruel group of warriors. Space and time are interconnected, one influencing the other. In *Ashes of Time*, we see how different characters visit an identical site, underlining the parallelisms in time. For example, Huang meets the Sunset Warrior's wife by a stream. In a later sequence, Ouyang meets her at the same location. What is interesting about these meetings is not the similarity of the location but how time invests one location with different meanings and significances. Space, then, in *Ashes of Time* becomes a way of focusing on the power of time.

In *Ashes of Time*, as well as in other films by Wong Kar-wai, there is a complex treatment of time that reinforces his vision of space, time and selfhood. The standard approach to time is to regard it as a continuous flow through which events move. Expressions found in common parlance such as 'time flies', 'the river of time' and 'time has slipped away' bear testimony to the fact that time is conceived as a continuous flow. The river is the normal paradigm of time. However, Wong Kar-wai seems to approach time differently. Events do not float in time giving rise to the categorizations of past, present and future. In his films, events need to be regarded as entities in space that are connected or related to each other spatially. Hence it is not helpful to talk of time in terms of unbroken flow. This idea that time is a continuous flow is only a linguistic metaphor that we have got accustomed to use in daily language as away characterizing time. To imagine events as items flowing along in a stream while we observe them from the bank is misleading. We need to rise above this misleading paradigm. Wong Kar-wai seems to be saying that we need alternate conceptualizations of time. It is in that spirit that he is focusing on the spatiality of events and how events are spatially related. The fragmentations, dislocations, discrepancies and disjunctures in the filmic narrative that we alluded to earlier could be usefully understood in terms of this alternate way of making sense of time. What this 'static' view of time points to is not the powerlessness or unimportance of time but its power and importance seen from a different angle and in relation to a different frame of intelligibility. The long periods of waiting and inactivity that characterize *Ashes of Time* are visualized through spatial images and tropes. Wong seems to dismantle the easy binarism that Kant posits between space as dimension of the phenomenon of external sense, and time as the internal form of perception connected to inward states.

The question of time is a widely discussed philosophical problem that has given rise to a tremendous volume of literature. However, in terms of our own immediate interests, two contemporary philosophers who could prove to be valuable and illuminating are Emanuel Levinas and Jacques Derrida. Admittedly, they are not the names that one would normally bring up in discussing philosophical issues of time. Nonetheless, in terms of the concerns of this chapter they seem to be highly relevant. For Levinas, the moment carries with it the idea of its exclusion from all other moments — the idea that moments are separate and monadic. In his view, time and sociality are inseparably linked. In his words, 'The dialectic of time is the very dialectic of the relationship with the other, that is, a dialogue which in turn has to be studied in terms other than those of the dialectic of the solitary subject.'4 Clearly, Levinas' explanation works within a phenomenological and religious framework. However, the broad thrust of his statement could shed valuable light in understanding the problems of the human experience depicted in *Ashes of Time* in that, however lonely, solitary and withdrawn a character may be, as indeed some in the film are, the full force of time is registered only through the recalling of interaction with others. In other words, the sociality of time is a condition of its experience. Just as much as memory is not personal but social, as has been pointed out by Maurice Halbwachs, so time too is embedded in sociality. As Levinas remarked on another occasion, 'Time is not the achievement of an isolated and lone subject, but that it is the only relationship of the subject with the Other.'5 The broad approach to time and memory in Wong's film gains greater resonance when we place it within the discursive frameworks formulated by such thinkers as Emanuel Levinas and Maurice Halbwachs. This might appear as if it is an unwanted intrusion of theory into the discussion of the film at hand. The interesting point about Wong's work is that it invites such excursions.

Wong Kar-wai's approach to time is inscribed in his style, visual rhetoric and representational strategies. He pays great attention, as any filmmaker should, to the construction and commingling of images. His images become sites of critical thinking and inquiry, at times spreading their aura throughout the filmic text. Let us, for example, consider a recurring image, that of the large and revolving birdcage. Ouyang sits in front of the cage and its shadows play across his face and those of other characters. This memorable image conveys to us the fact that many of the characters in *Ashes of Time* are trapped in their memories. This is an example of what Gilles Deleuze would call a time-image, an entity that is almost transnarrative in its effect. Deleuze draws an important distinction between what he calls movement-image and time-image. This distinction can prove to be of heuristic value in our understanding of the way time has been represented by Wong Kar-wai in this film. It is Deleuze's conviction that with the growth of cinema and its attendant technologies, the mobile camera resulted in the emancipation of the viewpoint and the prioritizing of time over space. With the development of montage, according to him, 'The shot would then stop being a spatial category and become a temporal one.'[6] Rather than merely following the characters in action, the time-image, as opposed to the movement-image, tends to promote critical reflection on the very task of representation itself. The time-image has a way of compelling us to think critically about time that was not to be seen in the movement-image, which basically focused on the relationships among images. This is what Wong Kar-wai is seeking to do in his films including *Ashes of Time*.

When Ouyang is sitting before the revolving bird cage, which stands as a symbol of time and its entrapping powers, the image provokes us into thinking about the predicament of the characters whose lives are depicted in the film. It has a significance beyond its immediate narrative value. This image constitutes more than an incursion into the consciousness of Ouyang. It becomes a site for the critical reflection on the meaning of the film. Here we have an example of a time-image that facilitates a larger re-imagining of the significance of the film. This image enables us to engage time in a more complex manner. Another example of this kind of time-image in *Ashes of Time* is the long shot of a lonely horse rider moving across the screen at a distance. This is also repeated many times in the film, provoking us to think about the solitude of itinerant swordsmen as well as the plight of those depicted in the film. It is more than a means of narrative propulsion; it becomes the site for reflecting on the plight of the characters and their complex engagement with time.

We can pursue further Deleuze's division of images as a way of comprehending the tangled relationships among time, memory, and image that are of great importance to the meaning of *Ashes of Time*. The movement-image tends to concentrate on the establishment of a coherent chronological order and a clear plot line based on the available concatenations of events that are often disorganized and scattered. The focus here is on objective time. The concept of time and memory enunciated by the French philosopher Bergson is relevant to this undertaking. For him, memory-image is the realization of memory in terms of our current preoccupations. In our attempt to recuperate shreds of memory from the past, we can basically adopt two strategies. First, it is possible to identify the moment in which we are interested in and offer it in the form of a memory-image. This is what happens in the case of a memory image when the past events are given orderly form and chronological coherence. Second, recognizing the fact that it is difficult to order events from the past in terms of current preoccupations, we need to focus on the non-chronological and non-coherent, and different processes at work in time. Hence it is of the utmost importance that we chart the multifaceted relations between the past and the present keeping in focus the differences, discontinuities and disjunctures. It seems to us that this is what Wong Kar-wai is doing much of the time through the organization of his imagery. Gilles Deleuze remarked, 'In cinema, Resnais says, something ought to happen around the image, behind the image, and even inside the image.'[7] This is what happens in time-images. They allow us self-reflexive thinking on time and its representation in cinema. Most of Wong Kar-wai's images betray a sense of both deficit and surplus. He once remarked that you can show change by not showing change. It can be said that movement-image relates easily to the logic of Hegel with its emphasis on dialectical structuring of images while time-image is closer to the thought of Nietzsche with its stress on narrative construction as opposed to mimetic desire.

Wong Kar-wai is a film director who is obsessed with time; one perceives this obsession of his in most of the films he has made so far. It is scarcely possible to think of another filmmaker in Chinese cinema who is so preoccupied with clocks as is clearly evidenced in, *Days of Being Wild*. This film opens with a question by the male protagonist to one of the leading female characters as to what time it is. She tells him the time. And he responds by remarking, 'It's one minute before three on April 16th 1994. You're with me. Because of you I will remember this minute. From now on we've been friends for one minute.' After that we hear on the voice-over a female voice saying that, 'whether he remembers me because of that one minute, I'll never know — but I've always remembered him. Afterwards he came every day. We were friends for one minute, then two minutes, soon we met at least an hour a day.' Similarly, in his film *Chungking Express*, a policeman in love muses on the specific hour when he will move from twenty-four years old to twenty-five, marking exactly one month after his girlfriend jilted him. He has an odd habit of buying cans of pineapples (his girlfriend's favourite) with the expiration date exactly on his birthday. If she does not call him on this day, he resolves to eat all the expired fruit and move on.

In *Ashes of Time*, too, one observes his deep interest in time both in the diegetic and performative aspects of the film. The diary-like monologues by Ouyang, the constant indexing of time, repetitions and duplications, the cinematography that catches the layers of meaning of frozen time and the weight of dead time on characters indicate this interest of Wong Kar-wai. The dialectic that he initiates between the vast and timeless sands in the desert, the waters in the ocean and clouds in the sky and the highly temporally and spatially determined interactions among human beings in cramped settings is also illustrative of this fact. Time, memory and space are intertwined in complex and interesting ways in this film. Wong points out that time is memory without limiting space. Consequently, to evoke memory is to confine time to a demarcated and specified space.

The interconnection between desire and time is also an aspect of time that figures prominently in *Ashes of Time*. It is evident, on the testimony of thinkers such as Jacques Lacan that desire defies clear and ultimate formulation because it is always already beyond our intellectual and representational grasp and desire itself becomes the object of desire. And like time, with which it shares many features in common, it is open-ended and resists closure. One senses this in *Ashes of Time* where time and desire are inseparably linked. In almost all of Wong Kar-wai's work, which deals with unrequited love and unfulfilled desire, there are no happy endings for the lovers in which their desires are satiated in the fullness of time. Instead, they remain unfulfilled, continually fuelling their desire and experiencing the torments of time. Like time, desire for Wong is insatiable and uncontainable. Many of the characters in

Ashes of Time experience this unpalatable truth. The pursuit of closure is a will towards overcoming and obliterating difference. The fact about desire and time, as the director of *Ashes of Time* points out, is that they depend for their existence on their difference from themselves.

Another aspect of desire and time which is closely related to this and which finds articulation in *Ashes of Time* is the fact that desire is the outcome of loss. The loss always returns as desire, and desire always desires that loss. We see this clearly in the characters of Ouyang and his former girlfriend, Huang, Murong Yang and the Sunset Warrior. Loss as a product of desire is related to time. It is time that activates the return of that loss in the form of desire.

There are, it seems to us, three broad approaches to the use of time in cinema. One is chronological time. Here the focus is on the representation of events as they occurred over time. In films that are organized according to chronological time, the narrative is clear, understandable, and, by and large, presents no major challenges to the viewers. The second is the category of psychological time. Here events are organized into a narrative structure not on the basis of how they happened over time but in terms of the importance attached to them psychologically by the protagonist. Filmmakers who are interested in exploring aspects of psychological realism in their works favor this approach. Filmmakers as different as Alain Resnais, Orson Welles and Ingmar Bergman seem to favor this approach. Thirdly, there is epistemological time. Here the ordering of events is accomplished not in terms of standard chronology or the importance attached to them psychologically and emotionally by the characters, but in relation to the way events follow a search to make sense of the chaos and the disorder of world. Some of the films of directors such as Jean Luc Godard and Michelangelo Antonioni display this predilection. Wong Kar-wai's films, it seems to us, fall into this category. For example, the narrative structure of *Ashes of Time*, with its complicated recreation of events mixing diverse time frames, follows an epistemologically determined trajectory. The beginning of the film is the end of the story. The narrative discourse of the film is constructed in accordance with a time-logic that is closely related to an epistemological search. If Wong Kar-wai is a film director obsessed with time, it is only the merest courtesy that we explore his obsession with all the available intellectual resources open to us.

9

Melancholia

Ashes of Time, like most other films that reward close attention, is many-sided and tends to provoke lines of inquiry that carry the investigators in different directions. Hence, in order to comprehend the full force of meaning inscribed in this film, one has to examine it from diverse vantage points and perspectives employing different concepts, analytics and methodologies. One such concept that we feel serves to illuminate the experience thematized in *Ashes of Time* is that of melancholia, personified by the character of Ouyang Feng around whom much of the action of the film revolves. The idea of melancholia is found in traditions of thought in the East and the West under different rubrics and categorizations. The way this phenomenon has been conceptualized in different traditions of thinking, understandably enough, varies significantly keeping in line with culturally sanctioned modes of knowledge production. In our attempt to press into service the idea of melancholia as a way of gaining access to the core experience configured in *Ashes of Time*, we have sought to draw on the Western tradition, most notably the writings of Sigmund Freud, Melanie Klein, Julia Kristeva, Judith Butler and Grigorio Agamben.

The word 'melancholia' is the Latin translation of a Greek word, which originally signified a mental disorder involving prolonged fever and depression. Sometimes it came to denote biliousness. Diverse disorders that were regarded as having their origin in black bile were generally designated as melancholic diseases. The word 'melancholia' began to be used widely in the seventeenth century, although from the fourteenth century onwards one can trace its use. Ever since the word gained wide currency, there have been various attempts to analyze it from diverse theoretical standpoints. Melancholia becomes important in understanding how psychological and social experiences produce each other.

The groundbreaking paper by Sigmund Freud (1856–1939) titled 'Mourning and Melancholia', published in 1917, is most relevant. According to Freud, there is a sense of similarity and difference between mourning and melancholia. Mourning can be regarded generally as the reaction to the loss of a loved person, or the loss of something abstract, such as an ideal. In the case of mourning, this feeling of loss and the ensuing grief is overcome after a certain period of time. What distinguishes melancholia from mourning, according to Freud, is the cessation of interest in the external world, the loss of the capacity to love, the tendency to refrain from most activities, lowering of self-esteem and the constant propensity for self-reproach. This diminishment of self-regard is absent in mourning. What is interesting about the self-reproachment is that it was focused against a loved object that has now been displaced onto the ego of the sufferer. When seen in this light, the self-reproachment and self-abasement of the melancholic constitute a conscious attack on himself or herself and an unconscious attack on the lost love object. It seems to us that the concept of melancholia as formulated by Freud opens an interesting window into the character of Ouyang Feng and others in *Ashes of Time*.

Freud argued that there are three conditions of possibility for the eruption of melancholy: they are the loss of the love object, ambivalence and the regression of libido into the ego. One can argue that these conditions are available in the experiential context of Ouyang Feng in *Ashes of Time*. The superego, too, functions in an important way in melancholia in that the internalization and the transformation of the lost object into a voice of recrimination. Hence, the voice of the sufferer is estranged as it becomes hypostatized in the voice of the lost object. While drawing a distinction between mourning and melancholia, Freud made the telling remark that, 'in grief the world becomes poor and empty; in melancholia it is the ego itself.'[1] This observation can provide us with useful insights into the motivations and behaviour patterns of Ouyang Feng.

The work of Melanie Klein, is equally important in our understanding of the concept of melancholy and its complex network of implications. Although she bases her analysis on the well-known essay of Freud that I referred to earlier, she goes far beyond it and complicates it by bringing in the notions of aggression and guilt in a way that Freud did not. She chooses to focus on the nature of the paradox endemic to melancholia; her emphasis is clearly on the nature and significance of aggression that is internalized by the sufferer. Melanie Klein sees the lost object as being introjected. However, there is a clear difference between the ways in which Freud and Klein conceptualize introjection in that Freud sees the act of introjection as a means whereby the lost object becomes a part of the psyche and a means of preserving it. On the other hand, Melanie Klein's investigations lead to the conclusion that the ego consumes the internalized object. Consequently, it is lost once again, this time as the object that had been introjected. This double loss exacerbates the agony of the sufferer more.[2]

While these observations of melancholia are useful for understanding the psychologies of Ouyang Feng, Huang Yaoshi, the Blind Swordsman, Ouyang Feng's former girlfriend and Murong Yin/Yang, the explications of Judith Butler can prove to be even more illuminating in gaining access to the wounded souls of these characters. In *The Psychic Life of Power* she makes the point that in order to map the full complexity of melancholia, one has to abandon the unproblematized and under-theorized understandings of external and internal space that are normally used in describing the nature of melancholia. The tendency to index psychic space by means of tropes of external and internal are themselves the product of melancholia. What she is seeking to establish is that the inner world that Melanie Klein pays so much attention to cannot be regarded as something antecedent to the process of self-bifurcation. For Judith Butler, then, melancholia can most productively be understood as the modality through which the mind is reconfigured as internal thereby enforcing the division between worlds that are internal and external.[3] This argument of Butler enables us to understand better the disposition of Ouyang Feng and the way the director of the film has sought to give cinematic expression to it.

Julia Kristeva, in her book, *Black Sun*, makes some useful observations on melancholia that have a bearing on the current discussion. She states that, 'there is no writing other than the amorous, there is no imagination that is not, overtly or secretly, melancholy.' This statement has a particular relevance to the experience portrayed in *Ashes of Time*. As Kristeva goes on to point out the reasoning of the melancholic seems to be as follows: 'I love that lost object' is what the person seems to say about the lost object, 'but even more so I hate it, the lost object; because I love it, and in order not to lose it, I imbibed it in myself, but because I hate it, that other within myself is a bad self. I am bad, non-existent, I shall kill myself.'[4] These remarks of Kristeva enable us to frame our understanding of the predicament of Ouyang Feng and other characters in *Ashes of Time* in more interpretively productive terms. Their situations might not conform exactly to the specifications of Julia Kristeva, but there is much in her exposition that is relevant to the experience of the film.

The Italian philosopher Grigorio Agamben has some interesting comments on the nature of melancholy that open up stimulating pathways of inquiry into the ambivalences and contradictions within the phenomenon of melancholia. According to Agamben, 'In melancholia the object is neither appropriated nor lost, but both possessed and lost at the same time. And as the fetish is at once the sign of something and its absence, and owes to this contradiction its own phantomatic status, so the object of the melancholic project is at once real and unreal, incorporated and lost, affirmed and denied.'5 The ambiguities endemic to melancholia are lucidly explained in these remarks. It might appear as though this discussion of some of the leading theorists of melancholia is somewhat tangential to the task at hand. This is not an unfair criticism. The reason we decided to include this discussion is that it demonstrates the richness, complexity and the relevance of melancholia as a hermeneutic device.

We can examine the character of Ouyang Feng against this backdrop of thinking. He was an agile and skillful swordsman and wanted to make a reputation in this field. His commitment to the pursuit of swordsmanship was so intense that he even neglects his girlfriend. Moreover, he did not tell her that he loved her. In frustration she marries his elder brother who is never shown in the film. This turn of events has a profound impact on his self-image. He decides to leave the White Camel Mountain and live in a vast desert alone. Ouyang Feng gives up the sword that he had loved so much before. Instead of becoming a noble swordsman, he now fashions himself into a cruel mercenary who gets other people to kill for money. There is a basic character transformation here. He gives up all the admirable goals and lifestyles he originally had to become a death broker. Moreover, he has lost the last vestiges of human warmth and generosity. When the young peasant girl with the basket of eggs implores Ouyang Feng to avenge the death of her brother, he refuses because she cannot remunerate him adequately. When Hong Qi is sick and his wife asks him to fetch a doctor, Ouyang Feng quite inhumanely replies that it costs too much. This basic character transformation in Ouyang Feng could be purposefully understood in terms of the idea of melancholy that we discussed earlier.

The film captures this sense of loneliness and self-abasement by drawing a sharp contrast between his sombre world and the vivid world of nature — the radiant sands, the variably bright skies, the lipid waters, whose beauty Ouyang Feng does not seem to appreciate or even care for. Moreover, the fissures and fault lines in Ouyang Feng's monologues suggest that his melancholia results in repetition and internal inconsistencies that one normally associates with melancholia. The blurring of character identities, the inmixing of character viewpoints, the contradictions within voice-overs, the dissonances between word and image, repetitions of place and event and the confusions of time highlight the melancholia which affects many of the characters in *Ashes of Time*. Ouyang Feng at one point in the film says, 'The harder you try to forget something the more it will stick in your memory. I once heard someone say if you have to lose something, the best way to lose it is to keep it in your memory.' These remarks by the main character of *Ashes of Time* jibe with the general tenor of thinking regarding melancholia proposed by Butler and Agamben.

Ouyang Feng may want to repress the fact that he has lost his loved object. However, what is repressed has a way of returning in interesting and complex ways. For example, all three female characters in the film remind Ouyang Feng of his former lover. He superimposes his repressed image of her on them, and the Sunset Warrior and Huang Yaoshi represent mirror images of him. Once again, the power of melancholia is vividly dramatized in the film. As a consequence of the melancholia affecting many of the characters in *Ashes of Time*, they feel uncomfortable in the world, seeing it as bereft of real human warmth and tenderness. It is a world abandoned by contentment. They retire to somewhere else, either physical or mental, in order to disengage from what obsesses them most, and seek solace in a world of fantasy. Unfortunately, no such world exists; even here the repressed reality breaks through and intensifies the melancholia.

The idea of melancholia is central to the meaning and structure of the film, and it has shaped the film's internal disposition in interesting and complex ways. As the characters in *Ashes of Time* struggle with their predicaments, we perceive how hope repeatedly seeks to create out of its own ruins the image of its own viability — a distinct performative element of the melancholic experience. The characters inhabit the language of loss, and the imperatives of loss are inscribed in the very thought processes through which they seek to master that loss. The strategy of withdrawing into the protected world of the interior, as is exemplified in the character of Ouyang Feng, only deepens the loss. The paradox of melancholia is that those suffering from it fail to recognize — and even when they recognize them, they resist — the very understandings and insights that could emancipate them from their imprisoning illusions.

A characteristic feature of melancholia is the deep ambivalence that accompanies it. Each of the main characters in *Ashes of Time* — Ouyang, Huang, Murong Yin, Ouyang's girlfriend and the Sunset Warrior — sees a disconcerting image of himself or herself in the mirror of disavowal. This is vitally linked to the semiotics of melancholia and the visual rhetoric of the film. The loss and reinscription of the object of cathexis, and the ambiguity of subject-formation are central. The contradictions between the aural and the visual registers, and the verbal and iconic registers, subtend this constitutive ambivalence. What Wong Kar-wai wishes to emphasize in his film is the fact that melancholia is not a name but a site, a site in which the mind fails to read itself. The tragedy of these characters results from their inability to comprehend the objective conditions of their lives and rise above them.

The idea of melancholia has inflected not only the themes of the film but also its poetics. The dislocation in the visual grammar, metonymic contiguities, syntagmatic linkages in the narrative, and the discrepancies between the aural and visual registers that mark the style of the film are manifestations of this melancholia. That the signature of melancholy is embossed in most of Wong's films points to the stylistic ambivalence that informs his work. Roland Barthes once remarked that cinema is protensive, hence in no way melancholic. What *Ashes of Time* and Wong Kar-wai's other films demonstrate is the power of imagination to challenge the conventions of cinema.

One of the effects of melancholia is to induce a sense of fantasy in its sufferers. This is clearly seen in the desires and behavioral patterns of many of the characters in *Ashes of Time*. The sense of fantasy that is inscribed in the filmic experience results from the decision of Ouyang to leave White Camel Mountain and retire to the desert. The desert becomes the site for action that deny inaction, and inaction that deny action in the film. The oscillation between stasis and kinesis that pervades the film is given intensity by the atmosphere of the desert. Ouyang's statement in the film that, 'I didn't see the desert until now' takes on an added burden of meaning.

The desert has always been a site of exile and self-denial. It is also a terrain of illusions and a terrain full of mirages. This relates to the melancholia of the characters in the movie in interesting ways. Ouyang enters the desert having deserted his girlfriend and human warmth and tenderness. As melancholics usually are, he is torn between self-abnegation and self-validation. His wish to erase his identity that results in a greater need for identity. As in the case of most melancholics, his memory of love and love of memory create a chiasmus that is replete with superimpositions and tensions that deepen his melancholy. There are, of course, different ways of reading the desert; Meaghan Morris points out how the desert can become 'a preexisting pile of texts and documents, fantasies, legends, jokes, and other people's memories, a vast imaginary hinterland'.[6] If so, *Ashes of Time* can add another layer to the evolving meaning of the desert.

In discussing the idea of melancholy as it relates to the diegesis of *Ashes of Time*, we have sought to draw on the vocabulary and axiomatics of psychological analysis. However, at this point it is important to enter one caveat. Very often, psychological studies promote inquiries into the deeper recesses that tend to ignore the play of manifest signifiers, treating them as mere pointers to elsewhere. In the case of Wong Kar-wai's films, such a move is resisted by the richness, density and compelling power of the manifest signifiers. The tension between the vision of psychological studies and the rich textual surface of Wong's films make psychological inquiries both fascinating and daunting.

10

Fragmentation

As we have attempted to emphasize throughout this volume, fragmentation is a defining attribute of Wong Kar-wai's films which inflects his themes as well as strategies of representation. It seems to us that fragmentation is pivotal to the way he looks at the world, tries to make sense of it and communicates it to us through his aural and visual signifiers. Wong Kar-wai's world is a world of ruin where fragments come to both undermine totality and reflect it. It is one of his artistic convictions that truth, if indeed we can grasp it, has to be grasped through the fragments in which it is hidden. We propose to examine Wong's valorization of, and approach to, fragmentation under the sign of ontology, epistemology, and aesthetics.

The numerous critics who have written on *Ashes of Time*, both praising it and criticizing it, and the general public that has responded to it have invariably focused on this inescapable quality of fragmentation. W. B. Yeats's famous line, 'the world is now but a bundle of fragments', has a deep resonance in the film. The lives of Ouyang, Huang, Murong Yin/Yang, the Sunset Warrior and Ouyang's former girlfriend are presented in a fragmented manner.

Wong does not attempt to attain a totality of vision of the characters, regarding such an effort to be an impossibility. The story is told through discreet fragments — fragments of time, fragments of space and fragments of episodes constituting the discontinuous narrative. Similarly, the visual poetics of the film is invested with fragmentary qualities; hence fragmentation is central to Wong's ambitions as a creative filmmaker. He seems to be saying that the only way in which we could apprehend truth is through its broken pieces, keeping in mind Adorno's slogan, 'The whole is false'.[1]

In a sense, Wong's films — whether they are set in contemporary Hong Kong, Argentina or in some unspecified period in the past — can be regarded as allegories of cultural modernity. Here we use the term 'allegory' in a distinctly Benjaminian sense as opposed to the common usage. Walter Benjamin opposes allegory to symbol, and draws attention to the centrality of fragmentation in allegory.[2] Allegory challenges and undercuts mimetic reflectionism by focusing on fragmentation and discontinuity. This allegorical impulse is clearly at work in the narrative discourse of *Ashes of Time*. Although it is a kung fu movie set in an unnamed historical period, the mood and ethos inscribed in the work are undeniably modern, displaying the uncertain grammar of modernity.

Let us first consider the ontology of fragmentation as Wong Kar-wai has inscribed it in his *Ashes of Time*. For him, the world never presents itself as a totality, a well-knit unity, because it is never so. Instead, it is seen as being constituted by fragments, broken parts full of discrepancies. One has only to consider Ouyang's monologue voice-overs to appreciate this fact. In other words, fragmentation is a part of the ontology of the world, and to impose a unity and cohesiveness upon it is to violate its nature of being. The stressing of the fragmentary over the total is not an act of will to power on the part of the artist, but the only way available to understand the world as it is. Let us for example consider the world that the four male characters in *Ashes of Time* inhabit. It is a world in ruins, replete with despair, uncertainty and incomprehension. Indeed, these attributes are not confined to this film alone; in Wong's other works such as *Days of Being Wild*, *Fallen Angels* and *Chungking Express* we see the same world in its appalling decadence, discontinuities and discrepancies. For Wong, the very condition of possibility that the world exists is marked by fragmentation. Hence, the ontological importance of fragmentation. Although for the purpose of analysis we can talk of ontology, epistemology and aesthetics of fragmentation as if they are three distinct entities, in point of fact they are closely interconnected, and this is certainly so in the case of Wong Kar-wai's films. With regard to the epistemology of fragmentation it seems to be Wong's conviction that the world cannot be known in terms of its totality, putative unity or harmoniousness. For him, it is an illusion to believe in that possibility. For him, the only realistic and meaningful way of understanding the world is through its brokenness and disjunctions. What Deleuze calls the 'belief in the world' has to be tempered by an appreciation of the endemic fragmentation of the world. To seek to capture a unified and integral world is to attempt to capture an originary and idealized space, which is, of course, an impossibility. The notion that one can understand the world in its totality leads to a belief in fixed centres and an Archimedian point of observation. Clearly such centres and vantage points are not available to us and Wong Kar-wai articulates this fact in almost all of his cinematic works.

Wong Kar-wai's categories for knowing the world and interpreting it put stress on dislocations, fissures, fault lines and the solidity of details, such as a candle, a scarf or a pair of shoes, as in *Ashes of Time*. For him, details are important and consequential as they contain within themselves the possibility of revealing patterns of meaning in the wider world. We are not sure whether Wong is an admirer of Siegfried Kracauer's writings or not.[3]

However, it is useful to remind ourselves that one of the recurring themes in Wong's early works is that the world is invariably torn apart, and that there is no totality or fixed centre and human beings have to make sense of the fragments of life before them without the benefit of some higher meaning to guide them. Heidegger once observed that in existence there is a permanent incompleteness.[4] It is as if Wong is seeking to reinforce this Heideggerian insight through his emphasis on fragmentation.

Wong Kar-wai sees the world as a fissured text just as much as his filmic texts are. One has to read the signs in the text that are often disconnected from each other and display no obvious affinity to commonly acknowledged references. An interesting point to bear in mind about Wong's privileging of the fragment in his understanding of the world is that the fragments have to be removed from their natural habitat. That is to say, they must be de-contextualized and rearranged in relation to other newly de-contextualized fragments. The reason for Wong's artistic choices in this film as well his other films grow out of his conviction that modern experiences (and *Ashes of Time* textualizes an experience informed by a modern structure of feeling) are disjointed, transitory, ephemeral, arbitrary and haphazard. For him the reality of fragmentation is the fragmentation of reality.

Another aspect of fragmentation in Wong Kar-wai's films touches on the complicated question of identity. Many of his characters in *Ashes of Time* have incomplete and unfocused identities. They lead, to use Baudelaire's phrase 'fluid existences'. The identity of one character flows in and out of another, creating a complex geography and an intricate symbolic space as in the case of Ouyang Feng and Hong Qi. One effect of fragmentation is that it calls attention to the fluidity and incompleteness of identities. What we see here is not identity as essence but identity as construction. The characters in *Ashes of Time* are straining toward images of identity but never reaching them. Ouyang, Huang and Murong Yin/

Yang are cases in point. When one seeks to construct identities out of fragments, the results are almost always fractured and decentered identities.

Let us consider next the way that Wong's views on fragmentation inform his film aesthetics. As a filmmaker, it is evident that he opposes absolutism and favors the resonance of detail. His narratives are marked by spatial and temporal dislocations and disparate juxtapositions that serve to highlight fragmentation. He is wary of narrating the stories of ready-made worlds and so instead offers counter-narratives and anti-heroes that call attention to the complex task of reassembling the world. As we have seen earlier in *Ashes of Time,* discontinuity, difference and digression are what his narratives are about. For example, when Ouyang tells us about his views on life, the narrative conveys the impression that it is imminently under a threat of disintegration. *Ashes of Time* is an attempt to read the world as a text with a complicated syntax full of ellipses and elisions and this is mirrored in the narrative structure and the visual poetics of the film.

Wong Kar-wai's aesthetic is not motivated by a mimetic desire but a representational impulse. Because of this, instead of reflecting the world, which is an impossibility for him as a filmmaker, Wong looked for ways and means whereby he could reconstruct it cogently and meaningfully, but, at the same time, also tentatively. This is tied to his epistemology which valorizes fragmentation. Wong's film poetics seek to stress the fragment over unity, and this is evident in his cinematic representation of the human body. Very often in *Ashes of Time* he focuses on fragments of the body — arms, legs, ankles, eyes and mouths — because for him the human body is not only an object of desire, but it is also something that can express anguish, pain and worry. The fragmentary depiction of the body is a way of articulating this aspect. The loss of wholeness of the body metonymically represents the loss of the wholeness of the self —

an affliction that affects many of the characters in *Ashes of Time*. The trope of fragmentation, therefore, is a vital building block in Wong's film aesthetics.

Let us, for example, consider a scene toward the end of the film in which Ouyang is seen in a candle-lit room with his former lover. One can hear their argumentative exchanges in the voice-overs. The sequence is represented through imagery that is rapidly spliced together and juxtaposed in startling ways. For example, close-ups of faces, the extinguishing of a candle, bold pans and shots from a hand-held camera create a sense of fragmentariness. It captures the spatial and temporal dislocations and the fragmentation that are dominant elements in the experience through striking rhythms and juxtapositions. One is left with the impression that every shot in this sequence reconfigures the spatial and temporal viewpoint. However, the resulting scene it is not represented in an unbroken and orderly way. Instead, the dominant impression is one of fragmentation that characterizes the entire relationship between Ouyang and his former lover.

The world that Wong Kar-wai repeatedly recreates is one of decadence, exhaustion, decay and ruin. A focus on fragmentation, rather than on totality, is a way of highlighting the contours of this world. In *Ashes of Time* it is as if a cruel and merciless storm has blown over the mental and emotional landscape of the characters and they are seeking to put together a new one with available fragments. This desire is reflected in the film's editing and the voice-overs.

At the beginning of *Ashes of Time* there is the Zen inspired statement to the effect that: the flag is not fluttering, the wind is not blowing and only the heart is shaking. Similarly, throughout the representational aesthetics of *Ashes of Time* another important Zen concept is expressed, namely, the idea of *'mono no aware'* or the transience of things and the sadness it generates. This Zen Buddhist aesthetic, which has influenced much of poetry and drama in Japan, seems to have influenced the visual poetics of this film which continually depicts the inevitability of fragmentation.

When we examine the text of *Ashes of Time*, we realize that fragmentation is not an academic or philosophical issue; it is vitally connected with the meaning of the film. The characters in this film are all victims of memory. They are grappling with memory not only to overcome anxiety but also to realize their identities which are imbricated with memory. Wong's point about memory is that it is not continuous and objective but presents itself in bits and pieces that are determined by subjective imperatives. Fragmentation is part and parcel of the experience of memory. Hence, the focus on fragmentation is perfectly in keeping with the logic of the human predicaments depicted in the film. Walter Benjamin, who has written so perceptively on the question of memory, drawing on the trope of montage associated with cinema, underlined the importance of 'detecting the crystal of the total event in the analysis of the small individual moment'.[5] On another occasion he remarked, 'Memory is not an instrument for the reconnaissance of what is past but rather its medium. It is the medium of that which has been lived out. Just as the soil is the medium in which old cities lie buried, whoever seeks to gaze more closely at one's own buried past must proceed like a man who excavates.'[6] One point about excavations is that the objects found come in fragments.

As we stated earlier, the world that the characters of *Ashes of Time* inhabit is a world in ruin. The world in ruin has no totalities and unities, but only fragments and broken objects. Hence, understandably enough, the visual style and strategies of representation in *Ashes of Time* tend to underline this fragmentariness. Indeed, the visual style of the film is an extension of its themes. The discrepancies between the images, abrupt spatial dislocations, temporal disjunctions, self-conscious camera angles, jump-cuts, time-lapse photography, visual contradictions and slippages that characterize *Ashes of Time* point to the functional significance of fragmentation.

The concept of *jianghu* that we discussed in an earlier chapter has a relevance to our current discussion of fragmentation. It is Wong's desire to turn this concept on its head and resist its authority. In this process, the idea of fragmentation is highlighted. As Stephen Chiang-kiu Chan, in an insightful essay on the filmic imagination of *jianghu* in contemporary Hong Kong cinema argues:[7]

> With *Ashes of Time* we are thrown into a world not of generic heroism but one where the erosion of all heroic values had just completed its transitional historical course; in this *jianghu* we have all tacitly accepted that neither the urge for unification or the values of coherence can be realized ... The world out there is no longer the moral, teleological or counter-hegemonic *jianghu* we are used to imagine, framed in spectacles packed and packaged with bloody tensions and melodramatic conflicts. Instead, everywhere we see patches of gloomy, fragmentary brownishness, where one may pause only to let a passing doubt go to rest on no totalizing sense of certainty.

Wong Kar-wai's indubitable focus on fragmentation does not, of course, imply that he is given to nihilistic celebrations of chaos and that he is unaware of the need to re-imagine strategic totalities if only to contrast them with the actualities of fragmentation. As Jacques Derrida once observed, since fraturedness is itself an appeal to some totalizing complement, it is no longer sufficient to construe anything as a fragment. One has to envisage the whole of which it is a part. Fragmentation and fracturedness do not necessarily imply chaos. Wong's focus of interest as a film director is not chaos but the absence of absolutism and unity. He has in mind an imaginary space of unity against which the fragmentation and ruin and the rubble of social reality could be purposefully remapped. His is a cartographic attempt at reassembling fragments and not a celebration of nothingness and brokenness. It is interesting to observe in this regard the statement by Maurice Blanchot:[8]

> The fragment, as fragment, tends to dissolve the totality which it presupposes and which it carries off toward the dissolution from which it does not (properly speaking) form, but to which it exposes itself in order, disappearing — and along with it, all identity — to maintain itself as the energy of disappearing ...

The relationship between the whole and fragment is complex. The whole is never the destiny of the fragment. The sign of fragmentation circulating in critical discourse offers us useful frames of intelligibility in understanding the intent of the film. Fragmentation is a way of dramatizing the disconnected syntax of despair — despair that, as we have indicated earlier, afflicts many of the characters in *Ashes of Time*. The fragments breathe in the proximity of what they have shattered, and embrace what they lack. As we had occasion to point out earlier, there is a constant complementary quality and tension between tradition and modernity in the film. Hence, Wong Kar-wai's wish to point out how fragmentation of sensory experiences is closely related to the march of capitalism and its concomitant inflection on sensibility. What is interesting about the fragmentariness in *Ashes of Time* is that ultimately it is, even more than the reflection of social ethos, a reflection of itself.

This discussion of fragmentation in relation to *Ashes of Time* should not mislead one to the notion that Wong Kar-wai is promoting fragmentation as a treasured virtue. On the contrary, his approach to fragmentation is shadowed by a pervasive anxiety and apprehension. It is not as if the idea of a unity never makes its presence in his mappings of reality. Indeed, there is an implicit unity that irrupts in his films, and it is one of effect. This unity is not one of axiomatics but of consequences. It emanates from the frames of intelligibility constructed contrapuntally by the film audience on the basis of the social and internal landscapes provided by the director. It is a unity after the event. The very spectacle of fragmentation reconfigured in *Ashes of Time* is underwritten by a vision that gains depth and definition in contrast to an implicit world of unity. This unity, reimagined by the viewer, is provisional. It could at any moment be displaced by a more persuasive one. However, until that transpires, one has to imagine a unity of effect; one has to counterpose the fragmentation that we have discussed, if only to explore the nature of fragmentation.

11

Response

Influenced by reader response theory in literary studies, film critics and theorists are increasingly coming to believe that the response of the audience is an integral part of the meaning of a film. Moving beyond the idea of the textual subject — amalgamation of Lacan and Althusser — disseminated by theorists associated with the journal screen in the 1970s, contemporary film theorists are seeking to call attention to the active role of the viewers and the historical subject in the construction of meaning. Hence in exploring the meaning of *Ashes of Time* it is not sufficient to restrict interpretation solely to textual meaning; we have to explore the ways in which viewers have invested it with meaning and significance. How viewers have responded to it over the years in different ways becomes a part of the growing meaning of the film.

Initial reaction to *Ashes of Time* when it was released in 1994 was one of bewilderment and disappointment — bewilderment because the audiences were not provided with a usable compass to navigate the uneven textual surface of the film, and disappointment because, instead of an action film with a heroic story associated with kung fu movies, the audiences got a film that was introspective and with long periods of inactivity punctuated by brief moments of suspenseful action. This was a hardly a kung fu movie in the sense that the average audiences were used to.

The adjectives commonly used to describe *Ashes of Time* when it was first shown were boring, confusing, tedious, quirky, pretentious, shallow, beautiful and empty. There were of course some who felt that *Ashes of Time* was an innovative film that extended the artistic horizons of Hong Kong cinema. Such voices however were few and far between. Over the years the attitude of audiences to the film seems to have changed in favour of the film, although still there are a substantial number who hold strongly negative views on the film. Having seen such works as *Chungking Express*, *Happy Together* and *In the Mood for Love*, some viewers were persuaded to take a second look at the film and found much to their liking.

Let us consider some representative views of the film when it was first released. For example, Paul Fonoroff in his article 'Nothing More Than Images of Beauty' in the South China Morning Post, 23 September 1994, said:

> An exquisite photo album masquerading as a motion picture, Wong Kar-wai's latest feature *Ashes of Time*, is as visually arresting as it is emotionally hollow. With a cast list that reads like a roster of who's who in Hong Kong cinema, a technical team representing some of the best talent in the industry, a budget of Hong Kong $40 million and two years in the making ... the results are a hundred minutes of some of the most beautiful tedium to ever grace the Cantonese screen.
>
> To understand the story, one is advised to read the synopsis in the publicity material. It gives a sense of continuity to Wong's screenplay and clarifies many plot points that are only vaguely alluded to on screen. Even with this as a guide, much remains muddled about the tangled web that intertwines a group of

frustrated, down-and-out swordsmen ... and the women who help to ruin their lives.

In a piece by Sek Kei under the title 'Brand Names Create Dummy Audience' published in Ming Pao on 22 September 1994, the following comment was made:

> In point of fact *Ashes of Time* cannot be termed a good movie at all. It neither meets the artistic requirements nor does it achieve popularity at the box office. It borrows the names of characters from Jin Yong's *Eagle-shooting Heroes*. Constructed on this base it tells a completely different story. There are some good points but these are handled in a very disorderly way. It only reflects the director's self-indulgence, self-enclosedness. The cinematography is too superficial and artificial.

In a comment published a day later in the same newspaper by Sek Kei under the title 'The Confused Malicious West', he said,

> Much has been invested in making this movie, but it turns out to be only a draft. It is fragmented and the characters are not fully developed. The setting is not very clear and the transitions between scenes are coordinated poorly. The dreamlike voice-over becomes important in the linkage of the movie. Apart from its music-video-like inset of images, it cannot be taken as a movie at all.

Not all reviews published at the time were as critical of the film. Some saw many positive elements in it. For example Li Cheuk-to in an article in the Hong Kong International Film Festival catalogue 1995 said,

> In his first stab at the swordplay genre it already bespeaks an ambition to redefine the genre and the way he subverts the conventional film language and narrative are more than what

ordinary audiences can comfortably receive. But from the perspective of creativity, *Ashes of Time* is undoubtedly the most astounding Hong Kong film from last year. It elevates a dreamlike voice-over to become a major structuring device, and is at once narrative and lyrical; it creates an ambiguous relationship between the monologues and the images which sometimes appear as brilliant illustrations and sometimes stand on their own to evoke emotions or different states of mind or being: it has a development that only captures moments and does not propel the plot forward ... These are extreme experiments almost without predecessors in Hong Kong cinema.

Over the years however, the critical opinion seems to have turned in favour of the film. Many discerning critics have found, as Ackbar Abbas,[1] for example, remarked,

> *Ashes of Time* too could be discussed in terms of its structuring of visuality, time, space, and affectivity. What is less expected is the uncompromisingly somber tone of the film, which the beautiful cinematography only tends to heighten. It is as if all the humour and lightness were concentrated on *Chungking Express*, leaving the traditionally extroverted, action-based martial arts film the task of telling a story about the weight of dead time ... The film does not obviously parody or ironize the conventions of the genre. Rather the implications of the genre are followed through to their catastrophic conclusions, giving us in the end the complex continuum of a blind space and dead time.

Esther Yau[2] remarked,

> In the realm of reinvention, filmmakers have turned out different versions of what one may call, for lack of a better term, experimental syncretism. The sword fights that book-end Wong Kar-wai for example exemplify unique movement — image sequences in high velocity with choreographed, kinetic

movements to create a heightened sense of spatial fluidity. Experimenting with cinematography (film speed, filters, lighting, and focus) and ways to visualize space and movement, Chris Doyle and Wong Kar-wai collaboratively assembled a different kind of cinematic visuality — one in which seductive images, erotic sensations, and electronic music combined to subtend the repeated motives of loneliness, longing, and memory.

The well known commentator on Hong Kong cinema, Stephen Teo,[3] remarked,

> The narrative effortlessly connects one strand with the next strand as each new character, via perfunctory links comes into focus, including a swordsman who is slowly going blind (played by Tony Leung Chiu-wai) and a beggar swordsman (played by Jackie Cheung), both pursuing vendettas against a gang of horse thieves. The various figures with their individual stories are threaded together as they meet with Ouyang in the desert and talk about their lives and loves ... The cohesiveness of *Ashes of Time* also stems from the film's remarkable look, which is nothing short of ravishing. Christopher Doyle's grainy colour photography imparts an impressionist quality, while the pastel lighting recalls motifs from Chinese paintings, pointed up appropriately by the desert location and other more temperate landscapes (creeks, ponds).

Tony Rayns, in an article published in *Sight and Sound*, January 2000, says that *Ashes of Time*

> remains Wong's magnum opus, an epically imagined panorama of 'turmoil in the hearts of men' to quote the opening caption.

In a short essay published on 17 May 1996, Lawrence Van Gelder called it 'mythic, melancholy and mysterious' and that it is 'a philosopher's movie'.

In their book on Hong Kong cinema titled *City on Fire*, Lisa Odham Stokes and Michael Hoover, speaking of *Ashes of Time,* say that it is 'one of the most complex and self-reflexive narratives of Hong Kong cinema.'[4] They go on to make the further observation that

> in contrast to the vicissitudes of human endeavour the camera eye establishes the breathtaking landscape as a permanent feature imprinted on the film, grand and timeless. Along the slow pan of the mountains, desert, and sky shown in the early minutes is repeated near the film's end; reddish-tinted waves are the opening image and reappear throughout. A poetic moment of calm water appears, the soft ripple of waves as liquid colour reinforced by a majestic soundtrack.

Larry Gross, writing in *Sight and Sound*[5] comments,

> The reversal of expectations — where a mode of narration is more powerful than what is narrated — occurs most forcefully in *Ashes of Time* ... in a complex coil of stories within stories, the same simple themes of romantic disenchantment are restated, revised, modified. You've heard of Wallace Steven's poem '13 Ways of looking at a Blackbird'? *Ashes of Time* gives you four or five ways for men and women to feel passionately for each other and remain unsatisfied.

And Curtis Tsui sees an almost postmodernist ethos informing the film.[6] He remarked,

> One should note as well that although the film is set during an undetermined medieval time period, many of its narrative elements are decidedly 'postmodern', a social condition which cultural theorist Fredric Jameson argues is the central characteristic of late capitalism, in which moral judgments are irrelevant or at least inoperative. Ouyang then is a practicing capitalist; he is apparently interested only in profit, and that single

interest has left him bereft of values, feelings, and emotional connections with others.

What we then observe is that over the years there have been critically important attempts to discover newer facets of meaning in the content and style of *Ashes of Time*, and to revise some of the earlier assessments of the film. *Ashes of Time* is a film that grows on you, and repeated viewings are necessary to appreciate its complex artistry. Through these repeated viewings, one begins to develop newer frames of intelligibility that facilitate the negotiation of meaning with the filmic text. In a Wong Kar-wai film, the viewer needs to become an active co-creator of the meaning of the film. For this to happen, the viewer must be able to construct a temporary unity offered by the diverse fragments, both aural and visual, and come up with frames of intelligibility on the basis of clues and hints offered in the filmic text. This is, often, not an easy task, because Wong does not always offer signifiers that have a clear reference. Hence this calls for active involvement on the part of the viewers, and one can easily ignore or miss out on some significant details.

As we stated at the beginning of this chapter, audience responses are a vital part of the meaning of a film, and this is certainly the case with *Ashes of Time*. With this in mind, we conducted an empirical study among university students in Hong Kong regarding their response to the film. We selected 64 students from the Baptist University, Chinese University and Hong Kong University and conducted open-ended interviews regarding their attitudes to *Ashes of Time*. The responses can be tabulated in the following way:

Excellent	5
Good	19
Average	25
Bad	11
Very poor	4

What we see, then, is that of the 64 respondents, only 15 had strongly negative views of the film.

These are some excerpts from the comments of those who had positive things to say about *Ashes of Time*:

> I like the film very much. It contains a moving story. A film is not a novel. The story has to be told visually. What I like most about the film is its visual side. By that what I mean is that the film has been made very carefully with excellent photography and captured the beauty of nature.

Another found the story interesting and easy to follow:

> I know that lot of people have criticized this film. One reason is that they [think] that the story is confusing. I don't think so. I found the story easy to understand and very interesting. The characters were real and we could believe them. There are reasons for the way in which the male and female characters behave in the film. The reasons can be understood from the film.

Some found the cinematography the real strength of the film:

> I think *Ashes of Time* is a very good film because of the photography. The scenes of the desert and the streams and the battle sequences have been photographed in a very original way. The film succeeds mainly because of the strong photography.

Some others felt that this was a revolutionary film in terms of both content and form:

> This film is a very revolutionary film, that is to say it opens a new path to making martial arts films. The characters in this film are not like the heroes we see in martial arts films. They are not real heroes but ordinary people with personal problems. The director

has used characters with problems and defects to show that it is possible to make different kinds of sword fighting films.

Those who were disappointed and disenchanted with the film naturally had many negative comments to make:

> I did not like this film. It is very boring. There is no real action. And most of the time people just talk. The story is very confusing. The director could have told the story in a more simple and interesting way. I expect movies to be entertaining. I was not entertained by this film.

Some were of the opinion that the director was playing some kind of intellectual game with the audience:

> Like many of my friends I did not find *Ashes of Time* interesting. The incidents don't flow very smoothly. They are broken up unnecessarily. I feel that Wong Kar-wai is playing some kind of intellectual game with the audience. I am not sure what that game is. But I feel that the main point about a film is entertainment, and trying to be clever is not the role of the filmmaker.

Some other respondents were unclear as to what the ultimate meaning of the film was:

> I found the story in the film uninteresting and also I was not sure about the meaning of the film. Is the director saying that our society is full of wicked or miserable people? Or is he saying that we all are doomed? I was not clear about the point of the film.

Another said,

> I could not get close to any of the characters. They were too different from me.

There were others who were unhappy with the film that felt that the filmmaker was trying to imitate Western models:

> I consider this film a failure because it did not interest me and it did not voice out any important philosophy of life. Although this is a Chinese film with a story that takes place in the past, the appearance of the film is very much like modern Western films. I think the director is too influenced by Western directors.

This is just a sample of the views, both positive and negative, expressed by a group of university students, and no more than that. It is undeniably true that the sample is too small to make definitive statements about the response to the film by the generality of spectators. However, the comments of the respondents, in some small way, help us to understand the diverse reactions engendered in a group of university students by the film. Clearly, the way in which some university students approached the film is not necessarily representative or reflective of the vast body of moviegoers in Hong Kong. However, their reactions place before us a cross-section of the views of the educated youth in Hong Kong regarding *Ashes of Time*.

12

Conclusion

We started out with the assumption that *Ashes of Time* marks a significant stage in the evolution of Hong Kong cinema. It is, in our view, a complex, self-reflective and visually remarkable film that rewards close and sustained attention. With this desideratum in mind we sought to locate *Ashes of Time* in its historical, cultural and conceptual contexts and to examine what we consider to be some important aspects of the meaning of the film, including the response of audiences.

In this concluding chapter, it is our intention to focus on two important dimensions of the film: its intertextuality and its social relevance. Wong Kar-wai's films, unlike the work of most other film directors, constitute an expanding and complex unity. In terms of theme, content, style, vision, style, narrative strategies and visual poetics there are echoes and reverberations across his works. For example, *Ashes of Time* can legitimately be termed a continuation of *Days of Being Wild*, although in terms of time and location they are clearly different. Statements made by characters in an earlier film echo in later films. A visual trope found in one film is given extended life in another. Sometimes these echoes are obvious and distinct and sometimes they are indirect as, for example, the echoes between the Sunset Warrior and Chang in *Happy Together*, both of them having prophetically meaningful problems with eyesight.

The intertextuality we are referring to is manifest, not only at the level of theme and experience, but also at the level of form and style. The agile camerawork, the dazzling play of light and shade, the visual disjunctions, the authority and intimacy of the many voice-overs, cross over from one film to another investing all of Wong Kar-wai's works with the indisputable signature of their author. Similarly, in terms of theme and content, agonies of unrequited love, fear of rejection, obsession with time, burdens of memory, non-chronological remembering of the past, isolation and solitude are shared by many characters in his other films. Hence, in order to understand the true dimensions of *Ashes of Time* we need to locate it in and connect it to Wong's total body of work.

Our attention should also focus on the film's social relevance. Wong is not an overtly political filmmaker. There are no political destinations to his films. However, there are political meanings inscribed in his work in the way that Michelangelo Antonioni's work carries political meanings. Has *Ashes of Time*, which is set in a period some ten or eleven centuries ago, any relevance to contemporary society? Does it reach out to make any comments and observations on modern societies? Some critics have sought to read the film allegorically, in the traditional sense of the term, and have seen in it a critique of the social disorientation prior to the 1997 hand-over as if the characters could be easily unmoored from their historical setting. Such readings, by and large, tend to be reductionist and mechanical, robbing the characters of their independent life. Rather than reading it in terms of a simple allegory in the traditional sense of the term, it might be more productive and fair to the director, to see the film as capturing a structure of feeling associated with the 1990s. Clearly, at the time of the production of the film, the day of hand-over was approaching, and there was a sense of unease, apprehension and confusion in the air. People were examining the past — the Opium War and the cession of Hong Kong, the lease of the New Territories, the Sino-British Joint Declaration, the Tiananmen Square incidents, Chris Patten's reforms and the responses of China — and now the hand-over, with anxiety. The polysemous Cantonese word *wuiguai* with its connotations of hand-over, re-union, restoration, return and decolonization aptly captures the mood of the time. This sense, we believe, has been textualized in *Ashes of Time*, not in terms of a moral fable or an allegory, but in terms of a shared 'structure of feeling' in the way that Raymond Williams first used the term.

According to Raymond Williams, a structure of feeling is the sense of a shared culture, a way of life that characterizes a community at a given period of time. The ideas, conventions, worldviews and apprehensions of a period are a part of the structure of feeling. Interestingly, he first developed this idea in his *Preface to Film* published in 1954. In it, he says that, 'in the study of a period, we may be able to reconstruct, with more or less accuracy, the material life, the social organization and, to a large extent, the dominant ideas.'[1] Clearly, Williams is talking of historical periods. We hope it is not too much of a misuse of his ideas to say that one might be able, in a more limited and narrow sense, to identify a structure of feeling in a work of art as well. In this case, it is a film. It is our conviction that *Ashes of Time* carries a certain structure of feeling that relates to the sense of confusion and anguish that characterized Hong Kong in the 1990s in the face of the impending hand-over. Hence, this is one way of seeing the relevance of *Ashes of Time* to the dynamics of contemporary Hong Kong.

There are, it appears, eight important aspects to this structure of feeling depicted in the film and experienced in Hong Kong of the 1990s. The first has to do with time. We stated earlier that the idea of time is crucial to the experience of *Ashes of Time*. People in Hong Kong in the 1990s were concerned with time — time that was running out as the hand-over approached. Hence the structure of feeling related to the obsessive concern with time found fertile ground in the imagination of Hong Kong people as they prepared for the hand-over.

The second aspect is the idea of fate and destiny. Speaking about *Ashes of Time*, Wong Kar-wai said that the characters were victims of a kind of fate. All of the characters were pulled along, willy-nilly, by an invisible and incomprehensible force. The sense of unease corresponds to the kind of feeling that was current at the time of the hand-over, and so this structure of feeling expressed by the film fit into the general mood of Hong Kong prior to their reunification with the Mainland.

Third, the idea of loss is central to the experience of the film; most of the characters encounter it in a particularly bitter form. The loss of the love-object is in a deeper sense a loss of one's own self. In discussing the importance of melancholy to an understanding of this film we discussed this topic at great length earlier. Here again, the pervasive mood of the film finds an echo in contemporary Hong Kong. The loss of the past, the loss of certainty, the loss of one's bearings had a great impact on the structure of feeling at the time. Moreover, this loss is vitally connected to the fragmentation that we discussed earlier. Fragmentation marks a loss — loss of unity, coherence, transparency, autonomy and so on. Fragmentation has come to occupy the status of a privileged frame of intelligibility in *Ashes of Time*. It is also connected to difference. Fragmentation is not difference, but it makes difference both possible and necessary. Wong grapples constantly with difference — difference within sameness. Murong Yang/Murong Yin is just one example of this proclivity. Loss, fragmentation and ambivalences of identity are vital keys to unlocking the meaning of *Ashes of Time* as they are for unlocking the mood that enveloped Hong Kong in the 1990s.

Throughout the film, as we discussed earlier, the human

experience is inscribed and circumscribed by the idea of melancholy. This has larger implications in terms of the structure of feeling in contemporary Hong Kong. Walter Benjamin's notion of 'left melancholia' is particularly apt in this regard. He conceptualizes this as a condition brought about by the valorization of a mistaken idea of progress in which the failure to seize opportunities and political formations are seen as unrecuperable losses. As Wendy Brown points out, 'Left melancholia thus represents a refusal to come to terms with the particular character of the present; it is a failure to understand history other than as "empty space" or progress. It signifies as well a certain narcissism with regard to one's past political attachments and identity that frames all contemporary investments in political mobilization, alliance or transformation.'[2] The notion of left melancholia, as glossed by Brown has a pointed relevance to the mind-set of the citizens of Hong Kong in the early 1990s.

Fourth, the spread of consumer capitalism and its impact on human relations was an issue that concerned many people in Hong Kong although they recognized the importance and inevitability of the spread of capitalist modernism early on. It was clear to them that Hong Kong became what it was largely due to this phenomenon. However, at the same time there was an understandable unease about the ultimate effects of capitalist modernity on human values and human relations. Wong Kar-wai reminds us that the fragmentation of sensory experience that the film stages is vitally linked to the imperatives of capitalist modernity. He is not a filmmaker who openly espouses human values in the way that a filmmakers such as Ann Hui do. Characters appearing in a martial arts movie are expected to represent noble and admirable values and an idealistic cast of mind, however in *Ashes of Time* they have succumbed to the lure of money and crass self-interest which resonates with this line of thinking. The rationality that dominates the film is, to use Habermas's favorite terms, not 'communicative rationality' but 'instrumental rationality'.³ In Wong Kar-Wai's films set in modern Hong Kong, the consumer society not only provides the backdrop to the action but also inflects individual relationships.

The fifth aspect is that *Ashes of Time* portrays a world drained of heroism. This fact becomes particularly evident when we contrast the world of *Ashes of Time* with the world configured in typical martial arts films that glorify heroism and its many facets. The absence of heroism and its replacement by a kind of petty self-interest can be readily understood by people living in modern Hong Kong. Hence, although the story of the film takes place some ten or eleven centuries ago, its mood, its ethos and its critiques have a direct relevance to the experience of modern Hong Kong. This interplay between the past and the present, the effacement and establishment of temporal markers serve to interrogate the idea of topical reference.

Sixth, many of the characters in *Ashes of Time* may be described as representing aspects of evil. However, even more than their predilection for evil is the undeniable fact of their vulnerability; they are wounded souls, battered by life, beset by uncertainties and leading solitary lives without real human warmth and meaning. Their evil nature grows out of their vulnerability. Even their propensity for occasional action emerges from their vulnerability, rather than from their strength. Once again, this sense of vulnerability fitted into the mood of Hong Kong at the time the film was made, as people in a spirit of introspection and with a certain measure of misgiving, explored what the future might hold for their society.

The seventh aspect is that, in *Ashes of Time*, Wong portrays a world inhabited by people who fail to connect with one another and are given to self-interruptions. It is a world that lacks a unifying architectonic — an overarching narrative authority that would invest it with a unity and coherence. All the characters in *Ashes of Time* share this fate. The failure to make connections with one another is intrinsic to their destiny. And this predicament faced by the characters in *Ashes of Time* informed the mood and the structure of feeling that prevailed in Hong Kong leading up to the hand-over. It was indeed a society that was uneasily divided within and against itself. Once again, we see how Wong's film reverberates with the pulse of the time. The contested understandings advanced by the film are inseparable from the topoi of disconnections.

Ashes of Time, which is very much of its moment, staged the intersections of hope and despair in captivating ways. This movie has complex implications for the re-imagining of Hong Kong after the hand-over. The day of hand-over was a day of decolonization, and for most colonies it would be a day of unambiguous celebration. For Hong Kong, however, it looked as if it was going to be a moment of ambivalence and uncertainty. Unlike other colonies, Hong Kong had no previous way of life to return to. It was troubled by the nagging question whether it was getting rid of one form of colonialism only to embrace another. It was caught between the contradictory pulls of Chinese patriotism, British imperialism and global capitalism. The local landscape, the richness of traditional Chinese culture and the global capitalist horizon converged in an uneasy union. As we stated earlier, the characters in *Ashes of Time* see despair as vast but in the end limited and hope as something that is limitless. It is this conviction that compels them to hold on to hope. On the other hand, they hang on to hope because hopelessness is so overwhelmingly threatening. The presence and absence of hope, as critics like Stephen Chan Ching-kiu have argued, is the informing dynamic of the cultural imagination of Hong Kong as it anxiously looks towards its future. Hope becomes the site for optimistic self-definition as well as troubling self-interrogation. Hope both erases and inscribes despair.

In this volume, we have aimed to read *Ashes of Time* in terms of our own particular interests, keeping in mind Maurice Blanchot's question about reading: To what extent it is possible to follow a text and at the same time to lose track of it, to be simultaneously the person it understands and the person who understands it? These phenomena are further complicated by the fact that reading cannot be separated from the 'field' in which the text operates as defined by the French sociologist Pierre Bourdieu.[4] According to him, cultural production transpires in a definitive social space that include artists, critics, producers, distributors, exhibitors, publicists, academics, journalists and others, and their voices have a determining influence on the meanings invested in the given cultural text. He calls this social space a 'field'. In the case of *Ashes of Time*, the meaning and significance of the film have been shaped by various segments of the field including critics, journalists, scholars, writers, the general public, film festivals, international commentators, researchers, university students and others. The actors in the field, in the way that Bourdieu uses the term, cannot be unlinked from the ultimate meaning and significance of the film, and its reverberating afterlife. Hence to understand Wong's film we need to keep in mind the specific contours of the field that it inhabits and how that field is related to the larger movements of society.

In conclusion, *Ashes of Time* relates in interesting and tangential ways to the mood of the 1990s in Hong Kong. In our analysis of the film, we have repeatedly stressed the importance of recognizing the inseparability of content and style in the film — how the film's images enact the themes. This has ramifications for the understanding of the contemporary relevance of the film. The imagery of the film with its emphasis on fragmentation, discrepant temporal and spatial registers, innovative camera work and editing, frequent use of jump-cuts, freeze frames, optical printing and so on, had the effect of making the viewer nervously conscious of time and space. Indeed, time and space were two topics that were uppermost in the minds of the people as they were mentally preparing for the *wuiguai*. The sense of despair, burdensome memory and ambiguity, experienced by many of the citizens in Hong Kong was experienced by many of the characters in the film. One aim of a film like *Ashes of Time* is the production of social intelligibility. The interesting question for Hong Kong is whether from the ashes of time, like a phoenix, a new society with its own vivifying cultural formations would emerge.

Appendix 1

Interviews

Wong Kar-wai Talking about Wong Kar-wai and His Movies

Audience reactions to Wong Kar-wai's movies are often contradictory. Some people like his movies very much and others don't. Days of Being Wild *received praise but also harsh criticism from audiences. Wong Kar-wai seldom reacts to these different assessments, thus, apart from talking about* Ashes of Time, *I will focus on questions regarding his movies and his favourite directors. In the end, these interviews will show that Wong Kar-wai does not like movies, but loves and enjoys the worlds created within movies. To Wong Kar-wai, movies themselves are not essential.*

Ashes of Time *is adapted from the characters of Jin Yong's novel,* Eagle-shooting Heroes. *But there aren't any elements of this novel that can be found in the movie, am I right?*

There is a relation. When we made this movie, we aimed at telling a story different from the book. At first, I was attracted by the names of two characters, Dongxie and Xidu, who, at the beginning of the design of the movie, we thought should be women. Later, we found out that there was no difference between buying the copyright of these two names and buying the entire book. Then, the idea of making this novel into a movie came to our minds. Another factor was that I enjoy reading this type of martial arts fiction, thus I was eager to turn it into a movie. The characters of Dongxie and Xidu impressed me most because Dongxie possesses natural grace but detests the world and its ways, something that we all thought was very cool. But I also had negative feelings about the selfish nature of Dongxie. The character of Xidu, on the other hand, appealed to me because he is a tragic figure.

At the beginning of the project I wanted to contact Jin. I thought when he first designed these characters he must have thought about their early histories but did not include it in his novel. In the end, it was good that I was unable to contact him because it allowed me to have more freedom in designing my characters. First, I imagined what these characters would be like when they were young. Then, I developed my own story that leads up to and concludes where Jin Yong's story begins.

So your interest in these two characters drove you to film a story with a historical setting?

Firstly, the genre is popular.

Was it popular even two years ago?

Yes. Secondly, since I had never made this kind of movie I thought that it would be fun.

When other directors have made movies with a historical background they usually used history as a means with which to satirize the present situation or because they wanted to film martial arts fighting scenes. What was your purpose?

I am not ambitious. I was simply trying to make a movie with a historical setting. It is actually very hard to make a movie with an historical setting and so I found an easy way out by handling it in a modern way. I did not pay attention to traditional social hierarchy, even though this genre can be very formalistic, such as each of the different social ranks having different manners. I thought it was ridiculous to spend time to investigate into history for details because, after all, they may not be accurate. You can never be sure whether the details extracted from your investigation are accurate or not.

While we were making the movie, we discovered one crucial point that we had overlooked. The preliminary concept was about Leslie Cheung's revenge. After reading some books on the theme of revenge in China, we were then alerted to the fact that there were many rules for one who decided to take revenge and it would take his character more than twenty years to complete this task. One thing that is never mentioned in most movies of this genre is travel. To travel to one location to another, one has to pass through many desolate places. Someone who seeks revenge may start to forget his language or start talking to himself. His determination for revenge may also be softened as time goes by. It is this passage of time that movies of this genre usually neglect.

Have you considered making a road movie with a traditional Chinese setting?

Originally, I wanted to make a road movie along the route of the Yellow River. It was just too difficult and it was also impossible for cast members like Leslie Cheung and Brigitte Lin to stand such a long period of shooting.

My colleagues and I were inspired by *The Searchers*, a movie in which a man spends years looking for another person. The protagonist experiences the passage of time as he goes through the process of searching. He has to sell his possessions to keep on going. This is a very good movie as it allows one to look into this dimension of life.

So that original idea turned into Ashes?

Because it was impossible to film a road movie, I set the movie in a specific space.

Is Ashes *about the feelings of the characters?*

The most important thing is feeling. I put into this movie my favourite story, a love affair between one woman and Dongxie and Xidu that has lasted for more than half their lives.

Does that mean in making this movie, you have filmed modern love affairs in the guise of a traditional Chinese story?

Some feelings are timeless. Until the end of this movie I did not realize the relationship between this one and my other movies. All of them are about being rejected and the fear of being rejected. In *Days of Being Wild*, every character has been rejected by the others for different reasons. It is fear that causes them to reject others, so as to eliminate the chance of being rejected themselves. Apart from this, the movie is also about how to react and overcome the rejection in the way that Maggie Cheung and Carina Lau's characters do. It is the same in Chungking Express. Maybe I have changed and that's why the ending of the movie is left open and there is not a definite outcome between the pair played by Tony Leung Chiu-wai and Faye Wong; they can accept one another as they are. *Ashes* is the most troublesome one. It is the sum total of the other three movies. In this movie, everyone is afraid of being rejected. After being rejected, they choose different ways to live with the rejection. Brigitte Lin's character finds consolation from her split selves through giving excuses. Tony Leung Chiu-wai's character uses death to reject everything. He is in a situation of no return because he loves his wife and yet he neither gives himself a chance nor forgives himself. In the end, he has to solve his problems in a destructive way. Leslie Cheung's character is in the same situation. After being rejected, he stays in the desert and never sets foot outside. The character played by Tony Leung Kar-fai drinks the wine of amnesia to escape from anxiety. All in all, my movies are about rejection, and the problems concerning escape. Some say that my movies are about time and space. They are wrong. My movies are really about myself. Thus, the characters in my movies live self-enclosed lives while hiding their own true feelings because of the fear of getting hurt.

Leslie Cheung's character in Days of Being Wild *is very indulgent person. At times, his influences on the other characters are very prominent. His character has the ability to control others' feelings. In Ashes, how are you going to present him?*

At the very beginning, I had the idea of having Leslie Cheung playing the role of Dongxie, but I came to think that such an arrangement might not bring any surprise to audiences because they would be expecting him to play a handsome man just like the one in *Days of Being Wild*. Because of this, I decided to have him play Xidu. Xidu nurses hatred in his heart. He is an orphan, and therefore knows perfectly how to protect himself and that the best method to avoid rejection is to reject others first. Pursuing such an attitude, he is always inside his own enclosure. No one can go near him. But eventually he realizes that this strategy does not work. He also realizes that if he misses his chance, he will not get another. His enlightenment is caused by the death of his enemy. Hong Qi also affects Xidu because Hong Qi is the one person who is not afraid of being rejected and sticks to what he believes to be right.

Leslie Cheung's character is trapped by his self-indulgence in Days, *while Andy Lau plays a man affected by his own insistence in* As Tears Go By. *Seemingly, they are moving towards a dead end. I can see that* Chungking *is a much more optimistic movie though it is also, like the other two, about mismatched people. At the end [of* Chungking*], I see the possibility of development between Tony Leung and Faye Wong ...*

When I was in the final stage of making this movie, I did compare it with *Chungking*. Because of its many dimensions, *Ashes* is actually a more serious, complicated and heavy film than *Chungking*.

In your previous movies, you have paid a lot of attention to lighting to create a suitable atmosphere. How about in this one?

The main feature in *Ashes* actually is the huge space. The most difficult task was to use candles as the only source of light as it would have been in the historical past. In the design of lighting, Christopher Doyle tried to avoid candlelight so as to have more freedom in filming. What's in front of the audience is a result of much later work in the studio. The visual effect is very satisfactory and I have to thank Ms. Liu from Universal.

Does the large number of characters mean that Ashes *is made up of many different stories?*

The role played by Leslie Cheung is the axis linking every story. Every character has a relationship with his. He is the centre of all of these happenings.

In every movie you bring to your audience something new. What about this time?

The newest thing is that I chose to take up a traditional genre. This genre is not too difficult to understand. The most special aspect of the film is the use of voice-overs. I first learned about this type of martial arts novel through the radio. I used to hide in my bed and listen to the radio when I was very small. Because of this, I included voice-overs in the movie. You can have an audience listen to my movie [instead of watching it].

Is this technique overused in local movies? It seems that many Hong Kong movies are now using this technique.

The voice-over offers another perspective to look into the incidents inside the movie. One has to control the use of it, otherwise it will come to dominate expressions. Bresson taught us to be precise. If everyone adopts his way, then the world would be very dry, just like taking vitamins and other pills instead of food. There should be more choices. For example, if you watch Satyajit Ray's movies, you will be stunned by their historical dimension. It is a different kind of beauty. It is not necessary for everyone to be molded by the same school.

The dialogue in your movies is very precise and accurately reflects the feelings and personalities of your characters.

I don't totally agree with you. The best dialogue is by Goddard. My dialogue is literal only. His is poetic.

Tam Kar-ming's Rhythmic Editing

In addition to being well known for using new concepts and filming techniques, Wong Kar-wai's movies also capture attention because of their editing. It took two years to make Ashes of Time *and the editing involved four editors: Patrick Tam Kar-ming, Hai Kit-wai, Kwong Chi-leung and William Chang Suk-ping. Tam worked out the overall frame of the story while the others trimmed the footage for a clearer outcome. In this interview we find out how Tam feels about being one of the editors and what techniques has he used.*

Wong Kar-wai is a very serious director. Although it is a very difficult task, I still enjoy working with him. Since last March, we have been working together for almost a year.

Wong pays extra attention to the relationships among characters and the acting of his actors and actresses rather than the arrangement of shots or the structure of the movies. Thus, his style of filmmaking is quite free. For example, when he is doing the outdoor scenes, he would film according to the environment of the place, and disregard the arrangement of shots and the mise en scene, even though I think that these tasks are the responsibility of the director. Because of this, I have to reconstruct the whole movie. Of course, Wong and I discussed the movie while I edited. The finalized version came out March this year but I have not yet watched the revised version.

Editing is making a sculpture. It is also a type of creation. I edit according to the 'feeling', the 'breath' and the rhythm of the movie. I'll cut those parts that don't fit in. *Ashes* is set among valleys, rivers and desert. It offers a strong sense of space and visual dimension as well as a sense of dryness and bitterness. It is different from *Days*, which emphasizes a sensuous atmosphere. Thus, more attention is put on the characters and their physical bodies. I'll analyse every scene and every shot and its mise en scene before editing. I edit according to the feelings evoked by the footage itself and the acting of the actors and actresses.

It is very difficult to describe editing in words. More precisely, there is no fast and slow editing, no long and short either. Editing moves according to the flow of the movie and its situation. I edit in accordance with my interpretation of these factors. After all, it is a matter of placing the actors and actresses and the desired feelings in a suitable position.

Chang Suk-ping's Costumes — a Return to Simplicity

Except the names of the characters, there is no sign of the original novel in Ashes of Time. *The designer can do whatever he likes regarding costumes because of the absence of a specific historical time as a backdrop. Together with the special visual effects created by the film, a strong sense of simplicity has been brought out, with an attractive result.*

In Ashes, *characters wear long hair without any decoration and their clothes are very simple. Where did your design ideas come from and why?*

I wanted to make the movie more real. The movie is set in the desert and the characters give a very strong sense of human presence. It was unnecessary to dress them in elaborate styles. The male characters all have the same hairstyle; their hair is put up. The four female characters are wearing the same hairstyle, too. There isn't a meaning assigned to such an arrangement. It is because people who live in such a place won't have someone to take care of their hair. Furthermore, it takes people several months or more to move from one place to another, so they don't have time to take care of their own long hair. In order to achieve a sense of reality, I had them designed in such a way. Because the director wanted to achieve a strong sense of texture, no sharp colours were used. Instead, wrinkled clothes of natural colours were chosen to match with the desert.

I don't have any experience in making such costumes because people usually ask me to create special things. This movie is quite different from the others I have worked on. In this movie, every character has only one set of clothes, for they seldom change their clothes. They look like painted characters in a traditional Chinese painting. They don't have many choices for even the cloth and the colour they use for their clothes. As swordsmen are always wandering from place to place, they don't have time to change their clothes very often. This movie is set in a desert, so it should be very dusty and dirty. Therefore, their clothes are different from those you would normally find in a movie with a historical background. For this film we wanted to try something new.

Could it be said that you present the real on purpose?

This is the most difficult part. Early on we had a design including the colours, texture of the clothes and hair ornaments that was quite different from what you see now. When we went to see the desert, we had to give up those designs for more simple things.

Was the colour of the negative changed?

Only to give a sense of texture. The negative was exposed with an E to C method, which makes it to look quite strange. The contrast is more obvious and that enhances the sense of texture and this contrast is even greater in the black and white sequences. For example, the yellowish color of the desert has been transposed to white and the shadows have become extremely dark. From time to time, there are some grey shades. It is quite interesting, especially when sharp red appears occasionally. We tried many types of negatives and many ways to create the desired effect. Filming it is different from exposing it. We wanted to create a special 'look'.

Frankie Chan — Making the Soundtrack with Fear and Trepidation

Wong Kar-wai commissioned Frankie Chan to make the soundtrack for Ashes of Time *because of their previous fruitful cooperation on* Chungking Express. *It is very difficult to create the background music for a movie with historical background without being too Chinese. Chan does not agree with the statement, as he found it was more challenging to create the soundtrack with only a glimpse of some parts of the non-edited version of the movie. That's what scares him.*

Ashes has a historical Chinese background but it has been entered film festivals abroad. It should be very Chinese but, on the other hand, excessive

Chineseness should be avoided to differentiate *Ashes* from other local movies with the same setting. This is what Wong Kar-wai wants.

I have only watched some of the unedited parts of the movie. Wong Kar-wai told me the story. To me, the relations between the characters are very intricate, especially between women and men characters. I started from this complexity to create my music out of this sense of emotion among these characters. Simple tunes are used as a backdrop for man-to-man scenes, like those between the characters played by Tony Leung Chiu-wai and Jacky Cheung, and Leslie Cheung and Tony Leung Kar-fai. These simple tunes are mainly played on a bamboo flute. Sometimes, it is even tuneless. More complicated musical arrangements are designed for the scenes in which women characters, such as Maggie Cheung and Brigitte Lin, are featured. I wanted to convey their inner feelings. This is done through an orchestration of Chinese and Western musical instruments. Vertical bamboo flute, erhu, gaohu, saxophone and guitar are the basic instruments for the music. The combination depends on different atmospheres in the movie.

The sound of the vertical bamboo flute creates a sense of loneliness and coldness that serves best as backdrop for the desert scenes. Northern erhu is used to enhance these feelings when Tony Leung Chiu-wai's character is fighting with his enemies. I used guitar to imitate pipa to describe the feelings of Brigitte Lin's character after she reveals her inner self. This adds a sense of sadness to the scene. There are scenes without music. Men's chorus is adopted for the scene of the killing the horse thieves. The chorus is singing melodies without any lyrics. When Brigitte Lin's character is deserted by the man played by Tony Leung Kar-fai, I use a man's solo to highlight the desolation.

I composed the music with a sense of fear, but it was also a challenge to me, just like taking a qualifying examination.

Translated from: City Entertainment *420 (Sept. 1994): 40–49.*

Appendix 2

Interactions Among Characters

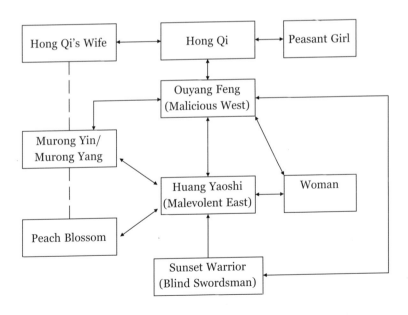

Notes

Chapter 1   Introduction

1.   Jacques Derrida, *Dissemination*. Translated by Alan Bass. London. Athlone Press, 1981.

Chapter 2   Background

1.   Ackbar Abbas, *Hong Kong: Culture and the Politics of Disappearance*. Hong Kong: Hong Kong University Press, 1997.
2.   Raphael Demos, 'Lying to Oneself.' *Journal of Philosophy* 57, 1967.

Chapter 3   Story

1.   Roland Barthes, *A Lover's Discourse: Fragments*. Translated by Richard Howard. London: Cape, 1979.

Chapter 4   Characters

1. Rene Girard, *Violence and the Sacred*. Baltimore: Johns Hopkins University, 1977.
2. Jacques Derrida, *The Ear of the Other*. Lincoln: University of Nebraska Press, 1988, p. 33.

Chapter 5   Narrative Structure

1. Lisa Odham Stokes and Michael Hoover, *City On Fire: Hong Kong Cinema*. London: Verso, 1999.
2. Henri Bergson, *Time and Free Will*. London: Allen and Unwin, 1910.

Chapter 6   Style

1. Ackbar Abbas, op. cit.
2. Pier Paolo Pasolini, 'The Cinema of Poetry.' In *Movies and Methods,* Vol. 1. Edited by Bill Nichols. Translated by Marianne de Vettimo and Jacques Bontemps. Berkeley: University of California Press, 1976.
3. Gilles Deleuze, *Cinema 2*. Translated By Hugh Tomlinson and Barbara Habberjam. London: Athlone, 1986.
4. Esther C. M. Yau (Ed.), *At Full Speed*. Minneapolis: University of Minnesota Press, 2001, p. 10.
5. Wong Kar-wai, *Nineteenth Hong Kong International Film Festival Catalogue*. Hong Kong: Urban Council, 1995.
6. Michel Foucault, *The Order of Things: An Archaeology of the Human Sciences*. New York: Vintage Books, 1994.
7. Marie-Claire Ropars-Wuilleumier, 'The Graphic in Filmic Writing.' *Enclitic*, Spring, 1982.
8. David Bordwell, *Planet Hong Kong: Popular Cinema and the Art of Entertainment*. Cambridge, Mass: Harvard University Press.

Chapter 7   Martial Arts

1. Stephen Neale, *Genre*. London: British Film Institute, 1980.
2. Lo Kwai-cheung, 'Transnationalization of the Local in Hong Kong Cinema of the 1990s.' In *At Full Speed*. Edited by Esther C. M. Yau. London: University of Minnesota Press, 2001.
3. George Bataille, *Essential Writings*. London: Sage, 1998.
4. Stephen Ching-kiu Chan, *The Limits of Utopian Resistance: Hong Kong in Radical Transit*. Typescript, n.d.
5. Mikhail Bakhtin, *Problems of Dostoevsky's Poetics*. Minneapolis: University of Minnesota Press, 1984.
6. Ackbar Abbas, op. cit.

Chapter 8   Time

1. Tony Rayns, *Sight and Sound*, October, 1995.
2. Jacques Derrida, 'On Reading Heidegger: An Outline of Remarks to the Essex Colloquium.' *Research in Phenomenology* 17, 1987.
3. Jacques Derrida, *Cinders*. Translated by Ned Lukacher. Lincoln: University of Nebraska Press, 1987.
4. Emanuel Levinas, *God, Death and Time*. Stanford: Stanford University Press, 2000.
5. Jacques Derrida, *Cinders*.
6. Gilles Deleuze, op. cit.
7. Ibid.

Chapter 9   Melancholia

1. Sigmund Freud, 'Mourning and Melancholia.' In *The Standard Edition of the Complete Psychological Works of Sigmund Freud,* Vol. 24. Edited and translated by James Strachey. London: Hogarth, 1953–1974.
2. Melanie Klein, *The Selected Melanie Klein*. Edited by Juliet Mitchell. London: Penguin, 1986.

3. Judith Butler, *The Psychic Life of Power*. Stanford: Stanford University Press, 1997.
4. Julia Kristeva, *Black Sun*. New York: Columbia University Press, 1989.
5. Grigorio Agamben, *Means Without End*. Minneapolis: University of Minnesota Press, 2000.
6. Meaghan Morris, *Too Soon, Too Little*. Bloomington: Indiana University Press, 1998.

Chapter 10   Fragmentation

1. Theodor Adorno, *Minima Moralia*. London: New Left Books, 1978.
2. Walter Benjamin, *One-way Street*. Translated by E. Jephcott and K. Shorter. London: New Left Books, 1979.
3. Siegfried Kracauer, *From Caligari to Hitler*. Princeton: Princeton University Press, 1971.
4. Martin Heidegger, *Being and Time*. London: SCM Press, 1952.
5. Walter Benjamin, *Illuminations*. New York: Schocken, 1969.
6. Ibid.
7. Stephen Chiang-kiu Chan, 'Figure of Hope and the Filmic Imaginary of Jianghu in Contemporary Hong Kong Cinema,' *Cultural Studies* 15, no. 3/4.
8. Maurice Blanchot, *The Writing of the Disaster*. Translated by Ann Smock. Lincoln: University of Nebraska Press, 1986.

Chapter 11   Response

1. Ackbar Abbas, op.cit.
2. Esther C. M. Yau, op. cit.
3. Stephen Teo, *Hong Kong Cinema: The Extra Dimension*. London: British Film Institute, 1997.
4. Lisa Odham Stokes and Michael Hoover, op. cit.
5. Larry Gross, *Sight and Sound*, April, 1995.
6. Curtis Tsui, *Asian Cinema* 7, no. 2, 1995.

Chapter 12   Conclusion

1. Raymond Williams, *Preface to Film*. London: Film Drama, 1954.
2. Wendy Brown, *Politics of History*. Princeton: Princeton University Press, 2001, p. 169.
3. Jurgen Habermas, *The Theory of Communicative Action*. Translated by Thomas McCarthy. Cambridge: Polity Press, 1987.
4. Pierre Bourdieu, *The Logic of Practice*. Stanford: Stanford University Press, 1990.

Filmography

Ashes of Time/ Dongxie Xidu (東邪西毒)

Hong Kong 1994

Director
Wong Kar-wai

Producer
Tsai Mu-ho

Screenplay
Wong Kar-wai

Cinematographer
Christopher Doyle

Editors
Patrick Tam Kar-ming
William Chang Suk-ping
Hai Kit-wai
Kwong Chi-leung

Art Director
William Chang Suk-ping

Music
Frankie Chan

Production Companies
A Scholar Films Co. Ltd. presentation of a Jet Tone Productions Ltd. production, in association with Tsui Siu Ming Productions Ltd., Beijing Film Studio and Pony Canyon Inc.

Chief Production Manager
Chan Pui-wah

Executive Producer
Jeff Lau

Associate Producer
Shu Kei

Production Supervisors
Norman Law
Tsui Siu-ming
Jacky Pang

Production Co-ordinator
Johnny Kong

Sound Recording
Leung Tat
Leung Lik-chi

Costumes
Luk Ha-fong

Props
Cheung Cheuk-wing
Shea Hin-hang
Cheung Bing-chi
Chan Kam-wah

Sound Effects
Ching Siu-lung

English Subtitles
Shu Kei
Linda Jaivin

Italian Subtitles
Maria Barbieri

Film Laboratory
Universal Laboratory Ltd.

Laboratory Technician
Lui Lai-wah

Subtitles
Fine Art Production Co.

Recording Studio
Mandarin Recording Studio Ltd.

Cast

Leslie Cheung (張國榮)	as Ouyang Feng (歐陽峯)
Tony Leung Kar-fai (梁家輝)	as Huang Yaoshi (黃藥師)
Brigitte Lin Ching-hsia (林青霞)	as Murong Yin/Murong Yang (慕容嫣/慕容燕)
Tony Leung Chiu-wai (梁朝偉)	as the Sunset Warrior (Blind Swordsman) 夕陽武士 (盲武士)
Maggie Cheung (張曼玉)	as the woman/Ouyang Feng's sister-in-law (歐陽峯之嫂子)
Jacky Cheung (張學友)	as Hong Qi (洪七)
Carina Lau (劉嘉玲)	as Peach Blossom (桃花)
Charlie Young (楊采妮)	as the peasant girl (孝女)
Bai Li (白麗)	as Hong Qi's Wife (洪七之妻)

Distributor
HKFM

Duration
95 minutes

Format
1: 1.85

Stock
Agfa Geveart

Selected Bibliography

A few of the following books and essays deal with Ashes of Time directly; others, directly or indirectly, give it a context.

Abbas, Ackbar. 1994. 'The New Hong Kong Cinema and Déjà Desparu.' *Discourse* 16, no. 3: 65–77.

———. 1997. *Hong Kong: Culture and the Politics of Disappearance.* Minneapolis: University of Minneapolis Press.

Berry, Chris. 1992. 'Heterogeneity as Identity: Hybridity and Transnationality in Hong Kong and Taiwanese Cinema.' *Metro* 91: 48–51.

Bordwell, David. 2000. *Planet Hong Kong: Popular Cinema and the Art of Entertainment.* Cambridge, Mass.: Harvard University Press.

Browne, Nick, Paul Pickowicz, Vivian Sobehack, and Esther Yau, eds. 1994. *New Chinese Cinemas: Forms, Identities, Politics.* Cambridge and New York: Cambridge University Press.

Cheuk Pak-tong. 1999. 'The Beginnings of the Hong Kong New Wave: The Interactive Relationship between Television and the Film Industry.' *Post Script* 19, no. 1 (Fall): 10–27.

Chu, Blanche. 1998. 'The Ambivalence of History: Nostalgia Films Understood in the Post-Colonial Context.' *Hong Kong Cultural Studies Bulletin* 8-9 (Spring-Summer): 41–54.

Collier, Joelle. 1999. 'A Repetition Compulsion: Discontinuity Editing, Classical Chinese Aesthetics, and Hong Kong's Culture of Disappearance.' *Asian Cinema* 10, no. 2 (Spring-Summer): 67–79.

Dancer, Greg. 1998. 'Film Style and Performance: Comedy and Kungfu from Hong Kong.' *Asian Cinema* 10, no. 1: 42–50.

Desser, David. 2000. 'The Kung Fu Craze: Hong Kong Cinema's First American Reception.' In *The Cinema of Hong Kong: History, Arts, Identity,* ed. Poshek Fu and David Desser, 19-43. Cambridge and New York: Cambridge University Press.

Doyle, Christopher. 1997. *Christopher Doyle's Photographic Journal of 'Happy Together', a Wong Kar Wai Film.* Hong Kong: City Entertainment.

Fitzgerald, Martin. 2000. *Hong Kong's Heroic Bloodshed.* North Pomfret, Vt.: Trafalgar Square.

Fonoroff, Paul. 1999. *At the Hong Kong Movies: 600 Reviews from 1988 till the Handover.* Hong Kong: Film Biweekly.

Fore, Steve. 1994. 'Golden Harvest Films and the Hong Kong Movie Industry in the Realm of Globalization.' *Velvet Light Trap* 34: 40–58.

——. 1997. 'Jackie Chan and the Cultural Dynamics of Entertainment.' In *Transnational Chinese Cinema: Identity, Nationhood, Gender,* ed. Sheldon Lu. 239–62. Honolulu: University of Hawaii Press.

——. 1999. 'Introduction: Hong Kong Movies, Critical Time Warps, and Shape of Things to Come.' *Post Script* 19, no. 1 (Fall): 2–9.

Frank, Bren. 1998. 'Connections and Crossovers: Cinema and Theatre in Hong Kong.' *New Theatre Quarterly* 14, no. 35: 63–74.

Fu, Poshek. 2000. 'Between Nationalism and Colonialism: Mainland Emigres, Marginal Culture, and Hong Kong Cinema, 1937–1941.' *In The Cinema of Hong Kong: History, Arts, Identity,* ed. Poshek Fu and David Desser. Cambridge and New York: Cambridge University Press.

——. 2000. 'The 1960s: Modernity, Youth Culture, and Hong Kong Cantonese Cinema.' In *The Cinema of Hong Kong: History, Arts, Identity,* ed. Poshek Fu and David Desser, 71–89. Cambridge and New York: Cambridge University Press.

Fu, Poshek, and David Desser, eds. 2000. *The Cinema of Hong Kong: History, Arts, Identity.* Cambridge and New York: Cambridge University Press.

Gallagher, Mark. 1997. 'Masculinity in Translation: Jackie Chan's Transcultural Star Text.' *Velvet Light Trap* 39: 23–41.

Glaessner, Verina. 1974. *Kungfu: Cinema of Vengeance.* London: Lorimer.

Hastie, Amelie. 1999. 'Fashion, Femininity, and Historical Design: The Visual Texture of Three Hong Kong Films.' *Post Script* 19, no. 1 (Fall): 52–69.

Havis, Richard J. 1997. 'Wong Kar-wai: One Entrance, Many Exits.' *Cinemaya* (October-December): 15–16.

Hong Kong Film Archive. 1997. *Fifty Years of the Hong Kong Film Production and Distribution Industries: An Exhibition* (1947–1997) [catalogue]. Hong Kong: Urban Council.

Hoover, Michael, and Lisa Stokes. 1998. 'A City on Fire: Hong Kong Cinema as the Cultural Logic of Late Capitalism.' Asian Cinema 10, no. 1: 25–31.

Jarvie, Ian C. 1977. *Window on Hong Kong: A Sociological Survey of the Hong Kong Film Industry and Its Audience.* Hong Kong: Centre of Asian Studies, University of Hong Kong.

Lalanne, Jean-Marc, et al., eds. 1997. *Wong Kar Wai.* Paris: Editions Dis Voir.

Lau, Jenny Kwok Wah. 1989. 'A Cultural Interpretation of the Contemporary Cinema of China and Hong Kong, 1981–1985.' Ph.D. diss., Northwestern University.

_____. 1989. 'Towards a Cultural Understanding of Cinema: A Comparison of Contemporary Films from the People's Republic of China and Hong Kong.' *Wide Angle* 11, no. 3: 42–49.

_____. 1998. 'Besides Fists and Blood: Hong Kong Comedy and Its Master of the Eighties.' *Cinema Journal* 37, no. 2 (Winter): 18–34.

Lau, Shing-hon, ed. 1980. *A Study of the Hong Kong Martial Arts Film.* Fourth Hong Kong International Film Festival. Hong Kong: Urban Council.

_____.1981. *A Study of the Hong Kong Swordplay Film, 1945–80.* Fourth Hong Kong International Film Festival. Hong Kong: Urban Council.

Law, Kar. 2000. 'The American Connection in Early Hong Kong Cinema.' In *The Cinema of Hong Kong: History, Arts, Identity,* ed. Poshek Fu and David Desser, 44–70. Cambridge and New York: Cambridge University Press.

_____, ed. 1991. *Hong Kong Cinema in the Eighties: A Comparative Study with Western Cinema.* Fifteenth Hong Kong International Film Festival. Hong Kong: Urban Council.

———. 1997. *Hong Kong Cinema Retrospective: Fifty Years of Electric Shadows*. Twenty-first Hong Kong International Film Festival. Hong Kong: Urban Council.

———. 1999. *Hong Kong New Wave: Twenty Years After*. Twenty-third Hong Kong International Film Festival. Hong Kong: Urban Council.

Lee, Leo Ou-fan. 1998-99. 'Hong Kong Movies in Hollywood.' *Harvard Asia Pacific Review* (Winter): 30–34.

Leong, Mo-ling, ed. 1985. *Hong Kong Cinema '84*. Ninth Hong Kong International Film Festival. Hong Kong: Urban Council.

Leung, Noong-kong. 1982. 'Towards a New Wave in Hong Kong Cinema.' In *Hong Kong Cinema '79*. Hong Kong: Urban Council.

Leung, Ping-kwan. 1997. 'From Cities in Hong Kong Cinema to Hong Kong Films on Cities.' In *Hong Kong Cinema Retrospective: Fifty Years of Electric Shadows*, ed. Law Kar. Twenty-first Hong Kong International Film Festival. Hong Kong: Urban Council.

Li, Cheuk-to. 1988. 'Cinema in Hong Kong: Contemporary Currents.' *Cinemaya* 1 (Autumn): 4–9.

———. 1996. 'Popular Cinema in Hong Kong.' In *The Oxford History of World Cinema*, ed. Geoffrey Nowell-Smith. Oxford: Oxford University Press.

———. 1988. *Changes in Hong Kong Society through Cinema*. Twelfth Hong Kong International Film Festival. Hong Kong: Urban Council.

———. 1990. *The China Factor in Hong Kong Cinema*. Fourteenth Hong Kong International Film Festival. Hong Kong: Urban Council.

Lo, Kwai-cheung. 1999. 'Muscles and Subjectivity: A Short History of the Masculine Body in Hong Kong Popular Culture.' *Camera Obscura* 39 (1996):105–25.

Lu, Sheldon Hsiao-peng. 2000. 'Filming Diaspora and Identity: Hong Kong and 1997.' In *The Cinema of Hong Kong: History, Arts, Identity*, ed. Poshek Fu and David Desser, 273–88. Cambridge and New York: Cambridge University Press.

Mintz, Marilyn D. 1983. *The Martial Arts Films*. Rutland, Vt.: C. E. Tuttle.

Reynaud, Bérénice. 1997. 'High Noon in Hong Kong.' *Film Comment* 33, no. 4 (July-August): 20–24.

Rayns, Tony. 1995. 'Poet of Time.' *Sight and Sound* 5, no. 9 (September): 12–14.

Sek, Kei. 1997. 'Hong Kong Cinema from June 4 to 1997.' In *Fifty Years of Electric Shadows,* ed. Law Kar, 120-25. Twenty-first Hong Kong International Film Festival. Hong Kong: Urban Council.

Stephens, Chuck. 1996. 'Time Pieces: Wong Kar-wai and the Persistence of Memory.' *Film Comment* 32, no. 1 (January-February): 12–18.

Stokes, Lisa Odham, and Michael Hoover. 1999. *City on Fire: Hong Kong Cinema.* London and New York: Verso.

Stringer, Julian. 1994. 'Hong Kong Cinema: Double Marginalization and Cultural Resistance.' *Southeast Asian Journal of Social Sciences* 22: 53–71.

Tan, See Kam. 1993. 'The Hongkong Cantonese Vernacular as Cultural Resistance.' *Cinemaya* 20, (Summer): 12–15.

Teng, Sue-Feng. 1996. 'From Bruce Lee to Jackie Chan: The Kungfu Film Carries On.' *Sinorama* (June): 28–35.

Teo, Stephen. 1994. 'The Hong Kong New Wave: Before and After.' *Cinemaya* 23 (Spring): 28–32.

_____. 1997. *Hong Kong Cinema: The Extra Dimensions.* London: British F&W Institute.

_____. 2000. 'Hong Kong Cinema: Discovery and Prediscovery.' In *World Cinema: Critical Approaches,* ed. John Hill and Pamela Gibson. New York: Oxford University Press.

Tobias, Mel. 1979. *Flashbacks: Hong Kong Cinema After Bruce Lee.* Hong Kong: Gulliver Books.

Tsui, Curtis K. 1995. 'Subjective Culture and History: The Ethnographic Cinema of Wong Kar-wai.' *Asian Cinema* 7, no. 2: 93–124.

Weitzman, Elizabeth. 1998. 'Wong Kar-wai: The Director Who Knows All About Falling for the Wrong People.' *Interview* 28, no. 2: 46.

Wood, Miles. 1998. *Cine East: Hong Kong Cinema Through the Looking Glass.* Guildford: FAB.

Yau, Esther C. M. 1994. 'Border-Crossing: Mainland China's Presence in Hong Kong Cinema.' In *New Chinese Cinemas: Forms, Identities, Politics,* ed. Nick Browne et al., 180-201. Cambridge and New York: Cambridge University Press.

_____. 2001. *At Full Speed: Hong Kong Cinema in a Borderless World.* Minneapolis: University of Minnesota Press.